D1205367

JESUS

Loyd Thornton 9-5-201q

JESUS

THE LIFE AND MINISTRY OF GOD THE SON—
COLLECTED INSIGHTS FROM

A. W. TOZER

MOODY PUBLISHERS
CHICAGO

All A. W. Tozer Excerpts © 2017
THE MOODY BIBLE INSTITUTE
OF CHICAGO

All rights reserved. No part of this book may be reproduced in any form without permission in writing from the publisher, except in the case of brief quotations embodied in critical articles or reviews.

All Scripture quotations by A. W. Tozer are taken from the King James Version.

All Scripture quotations in epigraphs are taken from the Holy Bible, New International Version®, NIV®. Copyright © 1973, 1978, 1984, 2011 by Biblica, Inc.™ Used by permission of Zondervan. All rights reserved worldwide. www.zondervan.com. The "NIV" and "New International Version" are trademarks registered in the United States Patent and Trademark Office by Biblica, Inc.™

Edited by Kevin P. Emmert and Linda Joy Neufeld
Interior and Cover Design: Erik M. Peterson
Cover art by Unhidden Media, unhiddenmedia.com

Library of Congress Cataloging-in-Publication Data

Names: Tozer, A. W. (Aiden Wilson), 1897-1963, author.
Title: Jesus : the life and ministry of God the Son--collected insights from
   A.W. Tozer.
Description: Chicago : Moody Publishers, 2017. | Includes bibliographical
   references.
Identifiers: LCCN 2016050199 (print) | LCCN 2017003737 (ebook) | ISBN
   9780802415202 | ISBN 9780802495358
Subjects: LCSH: Jesus Christ--Person and offices..
Classification: LCC BT203 .T69 2017 (print) | LCC BT203 (ebook) | DDC
   232.9--dc23
LC record available at https://lccn.loc.gov/2016050199

We hope you enjoy this book from Moody Publishers. Our goal is to provide high-quality, thought-provoking books and products that connect truth to your real needs and challenges. For more information on other books and products written and produced from a biblical perspective, go to www.moodypublishers.com or write to:

Moody Publishers
820 N. LaSalle Boulevard
Chicago, IL 60610

3 5 7 9 10 8 6 4 2

Printed in the United States of America

CONTENTS

PUBLISHER'S NOTE

A. W. Tozer was a man who encountered the living God, and he made it his life mission to help others know their Creator and Redeemer. And he was convinced that the only way to know God is in His Son, Jesus Christ, the very image and revelation of God.

The seventeen selections that follow are a small sampling of Tozer's writing on the person and work of God the Son. He covers topics like the Son's eternal nature, His oneness with the Father and the Holy Spirit, His incarnation, His mission to save lost humanity, His mediatory work in heaven today, His eventual return, and His everlasting reign.

What you will encounter in the following pages is a call to recognize Christ for who He is and to daily submit to Him as Lord and Savior. As Tozer put it, Christ is the center of all things. He is Creator, Sustainer, and Benefactor, the one who made us for His glory and to receive the bounty of His love:

> Out of His fullness we have received. There is no way that it can mean that any of us have received all of His fullness. It means that Jesus Christ, the eternal Son, is the only medium through which God dispenses His benefits to His creation.

Because Jesus Christ is the eternal Son, because He is of the eternal generation and equal with the Father as pertaining to His substance, His eternity, His love, His power, His grace, His goodness, and all of the attributes of deity, He is the channel through which God dispenses all His blessing. (Excerpted from chapter 3)

While these are the words of one man who died decades ago, they testify to the Son of Man and the Son of God, the eternal one, our source of Light and Life. Tozer would want you to focus not on him or his writing, but on the glory of Jesus Christ. May each selection in this volume point you to Him and inspire you to worship Him in awe and gratitude.

1

THE SELF-EXISTENT GOD

In the beginning was the Word . . .

JOHN 1:1

Any man or woman really sensitive to divine Truth discovers there is truly a kind of spiritual suffocation often felt in the attempt to wrestle with the opening verses of the gospel of John, or with the opening verses of Genesis, for that matter.

No man is really big enough and adequate in his own faith and experience to try to expound for others these key Bible passages. No man really ought to preach on the phrase "In the beginning . . . ," but the phrase is here and in our teaching as well.

We do our best to study and learn, and there is surely a deep and helpful message for us here, but we will still sense the feeling, expressed years ago by the poet, that "fools rush in where angels fear to tread."

We must meditate on the eternal nature of God in order to worship as we should. You know, I often refer to Frederick

William Faber, whose great adoring heart pressed into these mysteries during his lifetime in the nineteenth century, and he celebrated the vision of God's eternal self-existence in these warm and wondrous words:

> Father! the sweetest, dearest Name
> That men or angels know!
> Fountain of life, that had no fount
> From which itself could flow!
> When heaven and earth were yet unmade,
> When time was yet unknown,
> Thou in Thy bliss and majesty
> Did'st live and love alone.
> Thy vastness is not young or old;
> Thy life hath never grown;
> No time can measure out Thy days,
> No space can make Thy throne.

Brethren, surely this must be one of the greatest and grandest thoughts we can ever know: that it is the living and eternal God with whom we are concerned, and we acknowledge that only in God can there be causeless existence!

In this context, I confess a sadness about the shallowness of Christian thinking in our day. Many are interested in religion as a kind of toy. If we could make a judgment, it would appear that numbers of men and women go to church without any genuine desire to gear into deity. They do not come to meet God and delight in His presence. They do not come to hear from that everlasting world above!

Certainly we should be aware that everything around us has a cause behind it. You have a cause and I have a cause. Everything that we know is the effect of some cause.

If we could put ourselves into some special kind of machine that would take us back and back in time, back beyond the centuries of history, beyond the beginning of the creation, we might arrive at that point where there was nothing and no one except God Himself!

Imagining that we could erase history and everything in the universe, we would see in God causeless existence; God—self-sufficient, uncreated, unborn, unmade—God alone, the living and eternal and self-existent God.

Compared to Him, everything around us in this world shrinks in stature and significance. It is all a little business compared to Him—little churches with little preachers; little authors and little editors; little singers and little musicians; little deacons and little officials; little educators and little statesmen; little cities and little men and little things!

Brethren, humankind is so smothered under the little grains of dust that make up the world and time and space and matter that we are prone to forget that at one point God lived and dwelt and existed and loved without support, without help, and without creation.

Such is the causeless and self-existent God!

This God with whom we deal has never had to receive anything from anybody. There is no one and nothing to whom God has ever been in debt.

Some people have the brass to think they are bailing out the living God when they drop a ten dollar bill in the church offering plate on Sunday.

I do not think I exaggerate when I say that some of us put our offering in the plate with a kind of triumphant bounce as much as to say: "There—now God will feel better!"

GOD DOES NOT NEED ANYTHING

This may hurt some of you, but I am obliged to tell you that God does not need anything you have. He does not need a dime of your money. It is your own spiritual welfare at stake in such matters as these. There is a beautiful and enriching principle involved in our offering to God what we are and what we have, but none of us are giving because there is a depression in heaven.

The Bible teaching is plain: you have the right to keep what you have all to yourself—but it will rust and decay, and ultimately ruin you.

Long ago God said, "If I had need of anything, would I tell you?" If the living God had need of anything, He would no longer be God.

So, that was before the beginning. We are concerned here with that which the Bible calls before the foundation of the world.

We are told that in the beginning God created. We are made to realize that God does not lean upon His own creation.

If God needed help or strength, He would not be omnipotent and He would not then be God.

If God needed advice and counsel, He would not be sovereign. If He needed wisdom, He would no longer be omniscient. If He needed support and sustenance, He could not be self-existent.

So, as far as man is concerned, there was a beginning and there was a Creation. That phrase "In the beginning" does not mark a birth date for God Almighty. It means the point in time as we think of it when God ceased to be alone and began to make time and space and creatures and beings.

But we are not quite ready to leave that pre-creation situation, before the foundations of the earth were laid, when God dwelt alone, the uncreated Being; the Father in love with the Son, and the Son with the Holy Ghost, and the Holy Ghost with the Father and the Son.

God is the eternal God, dwelling in a tranquility that had no beginning and that can have no ending.

Now, you may note that I have not used the expression "the pre-creation void." *Void* is a good and useful word. When we do not know what else to say, we call it a void.

But before the Creation, God was there and God is not a void. He is the triune God and He is all there is. In His existence before the Creation, God was already busy; busy with eternal mercies, His mind stirring with merciful thoughts and redemptive plans for a mankind not yet created.

This is a very good place to read Ephesians 1:4: "According as he hath chosen us in him before the foundation of the world, that we should be holy and without blame before him in love." I am well aware that sometimes when I preach I really worry the Calvinists. I know, too, that sometimes when I preach I worry the Arminians, and probably this is their time to sweat.

BEFORE CREATION

Paul told the Ephesian Christians that we were chosen in Christ before the creation of the world. Someone will run me around a lilac bush and say, "How can it be that you were chosen in Him before the creation of the world?"

I reply with a question: "How can you explain a time when there was no matter, no law, no motion, no relation, and no space, no time, and no beings—only God?"

If you can explain that to me then I can explain to you how God chose me in Him before the creation of the world. I can only say that we must take into account the foreknowledge of God, for Peter wrote to his Christian brethren and called them "elect according to the foreknowledge of God the Father, through sanctification of the Spirit, unto obedience and sprinkling of the blood of Jesus Christ" (1 Peter 1:2).

The acts of Creation in the beginning were not God's first activity. God had been busy before that, for He must have been engaged in choosing and foreordaining before the foundation of the world.

I wrote a little editorial squib some time ago under the title "We Travel an Appointed Way." I pointed out that we are not orphans in the world and that we do not live and breathe by accident and that we are God's children by faith. I said that it is true that our heavenly Father goes before us and that the Shepherd goes before and leads the way.

Some dear man who was among the readers wrote to me and said, "I was brought up a Methodist. In your comments, do you mean this to be foreordination? That is what the Presbyterians believe. Just what do you mean?"

I wrote him a letter, saying, "Dear Brother: When I said we travel an appointed way, I was not thinking about foreordination, predestination, eternal security, or the eternal decrees.

"I was just thinking," I told him, "about how nice it is for the steps of a good man to be ordered by the Lord; and that if a consecrated Christian will put himself in the hands of God, even the accidents will be turned into blessings. Not only that, but our God will make the devil himself work for the glorification of His saints."

It has always been the experience of the children of God that when we walk daily in the will of God, even that which looks like tragedy and loss in the end will turn out to be blessing and gain.

I did not mean to go down that deep. I was just saying that our heavenly Father leads our way and that the steps of a good man are ordered by the Lord. I am sure the Methodist brother can go to sleep tonight knowing that he does not have to turn Presbyterian to be certain that God is looking after him.

By the way, I do not know how this illustration got in there, for it was not in my notes!

Now, once again to the record of the Creation, "In the beginning."

It is plain that God created matter—and that is not bad! Matter is that of which any physical object is composed and from matter we have obtained our words *material* and *materialism*.

I think a lot of people in our congregations get confused when some learned brother advises us that we must all join in a fervent fight against materialism.

Everyone looks around for the enemy but there seems to be no enemy in sight. If a man does not know what materialism is how can he be expected to join the battle?

The word *materialism* has become part of modern jargon. The created things that we accept as matter are all around us: things we can touch, smell, taste, handle, see, and hear. Things that yield to the senses—they are material things and they are not bad.

Materialism in its crisis form occurs when men and women created in the image of God accept and look upon matter as the ultimate. Of material and physical things they say: "These are the only reality. Matter is the ultimate—there is nothing else!"

"We must fight materialism" does not mean that everyone should get a sword and run after a fellow named Material and cut him down.

What it does mean is that we should start believing in the fact of God's Creation and that matter is only a creature of the all-wise and ever-loving God and that the physical things that we know and enjoy are not the ultimate; they are not an end in themselves.

In the Creation account, God had to have some place to put matter so He created space. He had to make room for motion so He created time.

We think of time as something wound on a great spool in heaven and that it rolls off for men faster than it does for women. Time is not like that: time is the medium in which things change. It is not time that makes a baby grow—it is change that does it. In order for change to occur, there must be a sequence of change. We call that sequence time.

And then God made the laws that govern time and space and matter. It may be an oversimplification here but in the law He established, God was just saying to matter: "Now, stretch out and let things move around."

Then, in the record, we see that God created life. He created life so there could be a consciousness of time and space and motion and matter. Then God created spirit, in order that there might be creatures who were conscious of God Himself. Then He organized the entire universe and we call it the cosmos, and thus we have the world.

Now, I suppose Creation is a great deal more complex than I have described here, and that it took longer than it is taking me to tell about it. But it was the beginning when God created the heaven and the earth. That was the beginning of human thought. That was where matter began, with time and space. That was where created life began.

Oh, how glad I am for the plain record concerning the living, loving, and creating God!

GOD'S ETERNAL LOVE

I do not think I could ever worship a God who was suddenly caught unaware of circumstances in His world around me. I do not think that I could bow my knees before a God that I had to apologize for.

I could never offer myself to a God that needed me, brethren. If He needed me, I could not respect Him, and if I could not respect Him, I could not worship Him.

I could never get down and say, "Father, I know that things are going tough for You these days. I know that modernism is making it tough for the saints and I know that communism is a serious threat to the kingdom. God, I know You really need my help, so I offer myself to You."

Some of our missionary appeals are getting close to that same error: that we should engage in missionary work because God needs us so badly.

The fact is that God is riding above this world and the clouds are the dust of His feet and if you do not follow Him, you will lose all and God will lose nothing. He will still be glorified in His saints and admired by all those who fear Him. To bring ourselves into a place where God will be eternally pleased with us should be the first responsible act of every man!

All of these considerations are based upon the character and worthiness of God. Not a man or woman anywhere should ever try to come to God as a gesture of pity because poor God needs you. Oh no, no, my brother!

God has made it plain that there is a hell, a place for people who do not want to love God and do not want to serve Him. The sadness and the tragedy of this fact is that these are human beings all dear to God because He created them in His own image. Of nothing else in the Creation is it said that it was created in the likeness of God.

Because fallen and perishing man is still nearer to God's likeness than any other creature on earth, God offers him conversion, regeneration, and forgiveness. It was surely because of this great potential in the human personality that the Word could become flesh and dwell among us. The only begotten Son could not take upon Himself the nature of angels, but He could and did take on Himself the seed of Abraham, as we are told in Hebrews 2:16.

We are assured in many ways in the Scriptures that God the

Creator does not waste human personality, but it is surely one of the stark tragedies of life that human personality can waste itself. A man by his own sin may waste himself, which is to waste that which on earth is most like God.

Sin is a disease. It is lawlessness. It is rebellion. It is transgression—but it is also a wasting of the most precious of all treasures on earth. The man who dies out of Christ is said to be lost, and hardly a word in the English tongue expresses his condition with greater accuracy. He has squandered a rare fortune and at the last he stands for a fleeting moment and looks around, a moral fool, a wastrel who has lost in one overwhelming and irrecoverable loss, his soul, his life, his peace, his total mysterious personality, his dear and everlasting all!

Oh, how can we get men and women around us to realize that God Almighty, before the beginning of the world, loved them, and thought about them, planning redemption and salvation and forgiveness?

Christian brethren, why are we not more faithful and serious in proclaiming God's great eternal concerns?

How is this world all around us ever to learn that God is all in all unless we are faithful in our witness?

In a time when everything in the world seems to be vanity, God is depending on us to proclaim that He is the great Reality, and that only He can give meaning to all other realities.

How are the great unsatisfied throngs ever to discover and know that we are made by God and for Him?

The answer to the question, "Where did I come from?" can never be better answered than by the Christian mother who says, "God made you!" The great store of knowledge throughout today's world cannot improve on this simple answer.

The leading scientists can tell you of their extensive research into the secrets of how matter operates, but the origin of matter lies in deep silence and refuses to give an answer to man's many questions.

God, the self-existent God, all-knowing and all-powerful, made the heaven and the earth and man upon the earth, and He made man for Himself, and there is no other answer to the inquiry, "Why did God make me?"

It is so important for us in these troubled days to be able to stand firmly and positively in this declaration: "Thus saith the Lord!"

Our chief business is not to argue with our generation, nor is it largely to persuade or prove. With our declaration, "Thus saith the Lord," we make God responsible for the outcome. No one knows enough and no one can know enough to go beyond this. God made us for Himself: that is the first and last thing that can be said about human existence and whatever more we add is but commentary.

REFLECT

1. How would intentionally recognizing God's eternal and self-existent nature impact the way you live your day-to-day life?

2. If God doesn't need anything, then why did He create us?

3. If God is eternal and unchanging, then what does that mean about His love for us?

2

GOD'S EXPRESS IMAGE

The Son is the radiance of God's glory and the exact representation of his being, sustaining all things by his powerful word.

HEBREWS 1:3

I wish I could comprehend everything that the inspired Word is trying to reveal in the statement that Jesus, the eternal Son, is the "brightness of his glory, and the express image of his person" (Heb. 1:3). This much I do know and understand: Jesus Christ is Himself God. As a believer and a disciple, I rejoice that the risen, ascended Christ is now my High Priest and intercessor at the heavenly throne.

The writer to the Hebrews commands our attention with this descriptive, striking language:

[God] hath in these last days spoken unto us by his Son . . . who being the brightness of his glory, and the express image of his person, and upholding all things by the word of his power. (1:2–3)

We trust the Scriptures because we believe they are inspired—God-breathed. Because we believe them, we believe and confess that Jesus was very God of very God.

Nothing anywhere in this vast, complex world is as beautiful and as compelling as the record of the incarnation, the act by which God was made flesh to dwell among us in our own human history. This Jesus, the Christ of God, who made the universe and who sustains all things by His powerful word, was a tiny babe among us. He was comforted to sleep when He whimpered in His mother's arms. Great, indeed, is the mystery of godliness.

Yet, in this context, some things strange and tragic have been happening in recent years within Christianity. For one, some ministers have advised their congregations not to be greatly concerned if theologians dispute the virgin birth of Jesus. The issue, they say, is not important. For another thing, some professing Christians are saying they do not want to be pinned down as to what they really believe about the uniqueness and reality of the deity of Jesus, the Christ.

CONVINCED ABOUT CHRIST

We live in a society where we cannot always be sure that traditional definitions still hold. But I stand where I always have stood. And the genuine believer, no matter where he may be found in the world, humbly but surely is convinced about the person and position of Jesus Christ. Such a believer lives with calm and confident assurance that Jesus Christ is truly God and that He is everything the inspired writer said He is. He is "the brightness of his glory, and the express image of his person." This view of Christ in Hebrews harmonizes with and supports what Paul said of Jesus when he described Him as "the image of the invisible God, the firstborn of every creature" (Col. 1:15), in whom "dwelleth all the fulness of the Godhead bodily" (2:9).

Bible-believing Christians stand together on this. They may have differing opinions about the mode of baptism, church polity, or the return of the Lord. But they agree on the deity of the eternal Son. Jesus Christ is of one substance with the Father—begotten, not created (Nicene Creed). In our defense of this truth we must be very careful and very bold—belligerent, if need be.

The more we study the words of our Lord Jesus Christ when He lived on earth among us, the more certain we are about who He is. Some critics have protested, "Jesus did not claim to be God, you know. He only said He was the Son of Man."

It is true that Jesus used the term Son of Man frequently. If I can say it reverently, He seemed proud or at least delighted that He was a man, the Son of Man. But He testified boldly, even among those who were His sworn enemies, that He was God. He said with great forcefulness that He had come from the Father in heaven and that He was equal with the Father.

We know what we believe. Let no one with soft words and charming persuasion argue us into admission that Jesus Christ is any less than very God of very God.

GOD BECAME FLESH

The writer of Hebrews was informing the persecuted, discouraged Jewish Christians concerning God's final and complete revelation in Jesus Christ. He spoke of the God of Abraham, Isaac, and Jacob. Then he declared that Another had come. Although made flesh, He was none other than this same God. Not the Father, for God the Father was never incarnated and never will be. Rather, He is God the eternal Son, the radiance of the Father's glory and the exact representation of His being.

Something has happened to the word *glory*, especially as it relates to the description of deity. *Glory* is one of those beautiful, awesome words that have been dragged down until they have lost much of their meaning. The old artists may have had something to do with it, depicting the glory of Jesus Christ as a luminous halo—a shining neon hoop around His head. But the glory of Jesus Christ was never a luminous ring around the head. It was never a misty yellow light.

I have a difficult time excusing our careless and irreverent attitudes concerning our Lord and Savior. I feel strongly that worshiping Christians should never be guilty of using a theological word or expression in a popular or careless sense unless we explain what we are doing. It is only proper when we speak of the glory of God the Son to actually refer to that uniqueness of His person and character that excites our admiration and wonder.

To those who love this One and serve Him, His glory does not mean yellow light or neon hoops. His true glory is that which causes the heavenly beings to cover their faces in His presence. It brings forth their worshipful praise: "Holy, holy, holy is the

Lord God of hosts!" The glory of the Lord is that forth-shining that gives Him universal praise. It demands love and worship from His created beings. It makes Him known throughout His creation.

It is the character of God that is the glory of God.

God is not glorified until men and women think gloriously of Him. Yet it is not what people think of God that matters. God once dwelt in light which no one could approach. But He desired to speak, to express Himself. So He created the heavens and the earth, filling earth with His creatures, including mankind. He expected man to respond to that in Him which is glorious, admirable, and excellent.

That response from His creation in love and worship is His glory. When we say that Christ is the radiance of God's glory, we are saying that Christ is the shining forth of all that God is. Yes, He is the shining forth, the effulgence. When God expressed Himself, it was in Christ Jesus. Christ was all and in all. He is the exact representation of God's person.

GOD'S EXPRESS IMAGE

The word *person* in this context is difficult of comprehension. Church history testifies to the difficulties theologians have had with it. Sometimes the person of God has been called *substance*. Sometimes it has been called *essence*. The Godhead cannot be comprehended by the human mind. But the eternal God sustains, upholds, stands beneath all that composes the vast created universe. And Jesus Christ has been presented to us as the exact representation of God's person—all that God is.

The words *express image*, of course, have their origin in the pressed-upon-wax seal that authenticated a dignitary's document or letter. The incarnate Jesus Christ gives visible shape and authenticity to deity. When the invisible God became visible, He was Jesus Christ. When the God who could not be seen or touched came to dwell among us, He was Jesus Christ.

I have not suggested this picture of our Lord Jesus Christ as a kind of theological argument. I am simply trying to state, in the best way I can, what the Holy Spirit has spoken through the consecrated writer of the letter to the Hebrews.

What is God like? Throughout the ages, that question has been asked by more people than any other. Our little children are only a few years old when they come in their innocent simplicity and inquire of us, "What is God like?" Philip the apostle asked it for himself and for all mankind: "Lord, show us the Father, and it sufficeth us" (John 14:8). Philosophers repeatedly have asked the question. Religionists and thinkers have wrestled with it for millenniums.

Paul preached at Athens and spoke of mankind's quest for the "Unknown God." He declared God's intention that mankind "should seek the Lord, if haply they might feel after him, and find him, though he be not far from every one of us: For in him we live, and move, and have our being" (Acts 17:27–28). Paul was speaking about the presence of God in the universe—a Presence that becomes the living, vibrant voice of God causing the human heart to reach out after Him. Alas! Man has not known where to reach because of sin. Sin has blinded his eyes, dulled his hearing, and made his heart unresponsive.

Sin has made man like a bird without a tongue. It has within itself the instinct and the desire to sing, but not the ability. The poet Keats expressed beautifully, even brilliantly, the fantasy of the nightingale that had lost its tongue. Not being able to express the deep instinct to sing, the bird died of an overpowering suffocation within.

God made mankind in His own image. He "hath set the world [eternity] in their heart" (Eccl. 3:11). What a graphic picture! How much it explains ourselves to us! We are creatures of time—time in our hands, our feet, our bodies—that causes us to grow old and to die. Yet all the while we have eternity in our hearts!

One of our great woes as fallen people living in a fallen world is the constant warfare between the eternity in our hearts and the time in our bodies. This is why we can never be satisfied without God. This is why the question, "What is God like?" continues to spring from every one of us. God has set the values of eternity in the hearts of every person made in His image.

As human beings, we have ever tried to satisfy ourselves by maintaining a quest, a search. We have not forgotten that God was. We have only forgotten what God is like.

Philosophy has tried to give us answers. But the philosophical concepts concerning God have always been contradictory. The philosopher is like a blind person trying to paint someone's portrait. The blind person can feel the face of his subject and try to put some brush strokes on canvas. But the project is doomed before it is begun. The best that philosophy can do is to feel the face of the universe in some ways, then try to paint God as philosophy sees Him.

Most philosophers confess belief in a "presence" somewhere

in the universe. Some call it a "law"—or "energy" or "mind" or "essential virtue." Thomas Edison said if he lived long enough, he thought he could invent an instrument so sensitive that it could find God. Edison was an acknowledged inventor. He had a great mind and he may have been a philosopher. But Edison knew no more about God or what God is like than the boy or girl who delivers the morning newspaper.

RELIGIONS HAVE NO ANSWERS

The religions of the world have always endeavored to give answers concerning God. Some religions declare that God is light. So they worship the sun and fire and forms of light. Other religions have suggested that God is conscience, or that He may be found in virtue. For some religions, there is solace in the belief that God is a principle upholding the universe.

There are religions that teach that God is all justice. They live in terror. Others say that God is all love. They become arrogant. Like the philosophers, religionists have concepts and views, ideas and theories. In none of them has mankind found satisfaction.

Greek paganism had a pantheon of gods. They saw the sun rising in the east and moving westward in a blaze of fire and called it Apollo. They heard the wind roaring along the seacoast and named her Eos, mother of the winds and the stars. They saw the waters of the ocean churning themselves into foam and named him Poseidon. They imagined a goddess hovering over the fruitful fields of grain each year and gave her the name Demeter.

Given such a pagan outlook, there is no end to the fantasies of gods and goddesses. In Romans 1, God has described the human condition that incubates such aberrations. Men and women, intrigued by their sin, did not want the revelation of a living, speaking God. They deliberately ignored the only true God, crowded Him out of their lives.

In His place they invented gods of their own: birds and animals and reptiles.

Often enough we have been warned that the morality of any nation or civilization will follow its concepts of God. A parallel truth is less often heard: When a church begins to think impurely and inadequately about God, decline sets in.

We must think nobly and speak worthily of God. Our God is sovereign. We would do well to follow our old-fashioned forebears who knew what it was to kneel in breathless, wondering adoration in the presence of the God who is willing to claim us as His own through grace.

JESUS IS WHAT GOD IS LIKE

Some are still asking, "What is God like?" God Himself has given us a final, complete answer. Jesus said, "He that hath seen me hath seen the Father" (John 14:9).

For those of us who have put our faith in Jesus Christ, the quest of the ages is over. Jesus Christ, the eternal Son, came to dwell among us, being "the brightness of his glory, and the express image of his person" (Heb. 1:3). For us, I say, the quest is over because God has now revealed Himself to us. What Jesus is, the Father is. Whoever looks on the Lord Jesus Christ looks upon all of God. Jesus is God thinking God's thoughts. Jesus is God feeling the way God feels. Jesus is God now doing what God does.

In John's gospel, we have the record of Jesus telling the people of His day that He could do nothing of Himself. He said, "The Son can do nothing of himself, but what he seeth the Father do: for what things soever he doeth, these also doeth the Son likewise" (John 5:19). It was on the strength of such testimony that the Jewish leaders wanted to stone Him for blasphemy.

How strange it is that some of the modern cults try to tell us that Jesus Christ never claimed to be God. Yet those who heard Him two thousand years ago wanted to kill Him on the spot because He claimed to be one with the Father.

God's revelation of Himself is complete in Jesus Christ, the Son. No longer need we ask, "What is God like?" Jesus is God. He has translated God into terms we can understand.

REFLECT

1. What does it mean that Jesus reflects God's glory?

2. Does knowing that Jesus is the express image of God change the way you view God?

3. How in your own search for God might have you forgotten what He is like?

CREATOR, SUSTAINER, BENEFACTOR

We have seen his glory, the glory
of the one and only Son . . .

JOHN 1:14

It is the truth that God has never done anything apart from
Jesus Christ. The stars in their courses, the frogs that croak
beside the lake, the angels in heaven above and men on earth
below all came out of the channel we call the eternal Word.
While we are busy presenting Jesus as Lord and Savior, it is true
that we have all received out of His fullness.

Now, some time ago I wrote in an editorial concerning Jesus
Christ that there can be no Saviorhood without Lordship. This
was not original with me because I believe that the Bible teaches
plainly that Jesus Christ is both Lord and Savior; that He is Lord
before He is Savior; and that if He is not Lord, He is not Savior.

I repeat: When we present this Word, this eternal Word
who was made flesh to dwell among us, as Lord and Savior, we

present Him also in His other offices—Creator, Sustainer, and Benefactor.

THE SAME GOD

It is the same Lord Jesus—and of Him John gives the faithful record: "Grace and truth came by Jesus Christ" (John 1:17).

I guess we all agree that the Law was given by Moses, and at this point I am not employing any contrast between Old and New Testaments. Any theological position that pits one Testament of the Bible against the other must come from a false theory.

The idea that the Old Testament is a book of law and the New Testament a book of grace is based on a completely false theory.

There is certainly as much about grace and mercy and love in the Old Testament as there is in the New. There is more about hell, more about judgment and the fury of God burning with fire upon sinful men in the New Testament than in the Old.

If you want excoriating, flagellating language that skins and blisters and burns, do not go back to Jeremiah and the old prophets—hear the words of Jesus Christ!

Oh, how often do we need to say it: The God of the Old Testament is the God of the New Testament. The Father in the Old Testament is the Father in the New Testament. Furthermore, the Christ who was made flesh to dwell among us is the Christ who walked through all of the pages of the Old Testament. Was it the law that forgave David when he had committed his great sins? No, it was grace displayed in the Old Testament. Was it grace that said, Babylon is fallen, the great harlot is fallen, Babylon is fallen? (paraphrase of Rev. 18:2). No, it was law expressed in the New Testament.

Surely there is not this great difference and contrast between Old and New Testaments that many seem to assume. God never pits the Father against the Son. He never pits the Old Testament against the New. The only contrast here is between all that Moses could do and all that Jesus Christ can do. The Law was given by Moses—that was all that Moses could do. Moses was not the channel through which God dispensed His grace. God chose His only begotten Son as the channel for His grace and truth, for John witnesses that grace and truth came by Jesus Christ.

All that Moses could do was to command righteousness. In contrast, only Jesus Christ produces righteousness. All that Moses could do was to forbid us to sin. In contrast, Jesus Christ came to save us from sin. Moses could not save, but Jesus Christ is both Lord and Savior.

Grace came through Jesus Christ before Mary wept in the manger stall in Bethlehem. It was the grace of God in Christ that saved the human race from extinction when our first parents sinned in the garden. It was the grace of God in Jesus Christ yet to be born that saved the eight persons when the flood covered the earth. It was the grace of God in Jesus Christ yet to be born but existing in pre-incarnation glory that forgave David when he sinned, that forgave Abraham when he lied. It was the grace of God that enabled Abraham to pray God down to ten when He was threatening to destroy Sodom. God forgave Israel time and time again. It was the grace of God in Christ prior to the incarnation that made God say, "I have risen early in the morning and stretched out my hands unto you!"

BEHOLDING HIS GLORY

The apostle John speaks for all of us also when he writes of the eternal Son and reminds us that we beheld his glory. It is right that we should inquire, "What was this glory? Was it the glory of His works?"

Jesus was not only a worker—He was a wonder worker!

Every part of nature had to yield to Him and His authority. He turned the water into wine and many people miss the point of His power and authority and argue about the difference between grape juice and wine. It mattered little—He turned water into wine. It was a miracle.

When our Lord came to the sick, He healed them. When He came to the devil-possessed, He commanded the devils to go out. When our Lord stood on the rocking deck of a tiny boat tossed by fierce winds and giant waves, He spoke to the water and rebuked the wind and there came a great calm.

Everything our Lord did was meaningful in the display of His eternal glory.

Think of the tenderness and compassion of the Lord Jesus when He raised the boy and gave him back to his widowed mother en route to the graveyard.

Think of the glory in His tenderness when He raised the little daughter of Jairus and restored her to her father's love and care. I think Jesus probably smiled at that little girl after calling her back from her death sleep and said, "Sit up, daughter. Time to go to school." You called your children when it was school time. I am sure Jesus used the same simple language of tenderness.

The works of our Lord were always dramatic works. Always

they were amazing works. We wonder if John had these things in mind when he said, "We beheld his glory," but I think not. I think John had a much greater glory in mind.

We can never know all of the wonderful works of healing and mercy that Jesus performed while on the earth, but we should fix our eyes on His glory, which was far greater than the miracles and works of wonder.

OF HIS FULLNESS

The Bible teaches so clearly and so consistently what John proclaims in the first chapter of his gospel: "And of his fulness have all we received, and grace for grace" (John 1:16).

Out of His fullness we have received. There is no way that it can mean that any of us have received all of His fullness. It means that Jesus Christ, the eternal Son, is the only medium through which God dispenses His benefits to His creation.

Because Jesus Christ is the eternal Son, because He is of the eternal generation and equal with the Father as pertaining to His substance, His eternity, His love, His power, His grace, His goodness, and all of the attributes of deity, He is the channel through which God dispenses all His blessing.

If you could ask the deer that goes quietly down to the edge of the lake for a refreshing drink, "Have you received of the fullness of the lake?" the answer would be: "Yes and no. I am full from the lake but I have not received the fullness of the lake. I did not drink the lake. I only drank what I could hold of the lake."

And so, of His fullness, out of the fullness of God, He has given us grace upon grace according to our need, and it is all through Jesus Christ, our Lord. When He speaks, when He provides, while He sustains, it is because it can be said that He upholds all things by the Word of His power and in Him all things consist.

Now, here is a thought I had one day: it could have been very easy for God to have loved us and never told us. God could have been merciful toward us and never revealed it. We know that among humans it is possible for us to feel deeply and still tell no one. It is possible to have fine intentions and never make them known to anyone.

The Scriptures say that "no man hath seen God at any time, the only begotten Son, which is in the bosom of the Father, he hath declared him" (John 1:18).

The eternal Son came to tell us what the silence never told us. He came to tell us what not even Moses could tell us. He came to tell us and to show us that God loves us and that He constantly cares for us. He came to tell us that God has a gracious plan and that He is carrying out that plan. Before it is all finished and consummated, there will be a multitude that no man can number, redeemed, out of every tongue and tribe and nation.

That is what He has told us about the Father God. He has set Him forth. He has revealed Him—His being, His love, His mercy, His grace, His redemptive intention, His saving intention.

He has declared it all. He has given us grace upon grace. Now we have only to turn and believe and accept and take and follow. All is ours if we will receive because the Word was made flesh, and dwelt among us!

REFLECT

1. What implications does Christ's lordship, as Creator of the universe, have for your life?

2. Does knowing that Jesus is the same God as the God of the Old Testament change your perception of God the Father?

3. If there is no opposition between the Old and New Testaments, what does that say about the relationship between the Father and the Son?

4. How have you received grace from Jesus? In what ways does Jesus want you to receive His grace in your life right now?

THE REVELATION
OF GOD

. . . in these last days he has spoken to us by his Son.

HEBREWS 1:2

When the author of Hebrews wrote to declare that "in these last days" God was speaking through His Son, he reminded us that for thousands of years God had been speaking in many ways. Actually, there had been some 4,000 years of human history during which God had been speaking to the human race. It was a race that had separated itself from God, hiding in the garden of Eden and holding itself incognito ever since.

For most people in the first century of the Christian era, God was only a tradition. Some fondled their man-made gods. Some had ideas of worship and even built altars. Some mumbled incantations and said prayers. But they were alienated from the true God. Although they were made in the image of God, they had rejected their Creator, casting in their lot with mortality.

That situation might have continued until man or nature or both failed and were no more. But God in love and wisdom came once more. He came to speak, revealing Himself this time through His eternal Son. It is because of the coming of Jesus into the world that we now look back on the revelation in the Old Testament as fragmentary and incomplete. We could say that the Old Testament is like a house without doors and windows. Not until the carpenters cut in doors and windows can that house become a worthy, satisfying residence.

Years ago my family and I enjoyed Christian fellowship with a Jewish medical doctor who had come to personal faith in Jesus, the Savior and Messiah. He gladly discussed with me his previous participation in Sabbath services in the synagogue. Often he had been asked to read from the Old Testament Scriptures.

"I often think back on those years of reading from the Old Testament," he told me. "I had the haunting sense that it was good and true. I knew it explained the history of my people. But I had the feeling that something was missing." Then, with a beautiful, radiant smile he added, "When I found Jesus as my personal Savior and Messiah, I found Him to be the One to whom the Old Testament was in fact pointing. I found Him to be the answer to my completion as a Jew, as a person, and as a believer."

Whether Jew or Gentile, we were made originally in God's image, and the revelation of God by His Spirit is a necessity. An understanding of the Word of God must come from the same Spirit who provided its inspiration.

GOD'S MESSAGE IN THE PAST

The letter to the Hebrews was written to confirm the early Jewish Christians in their faith in Jesus, the Messiah-Savior. The writer takes a recurring theme that Jesus Christ is better because He is superior. Jesus Christ is the ultimate Word from God!

This is a reassuring, strengthening message to us in our day. Hebrews lets us know that while our Christian faith surely was foreshadowed in and grew out of Judaism, it was not and is not dependent on Judaism. The words of our Lord Jesus Christ, spoken while He was here on earth, still speak to us with spiritual authority. At one time He reminded His disciples that new wine must never be put in old, inelastic wineskins. The parable was patent: the old religious forms and traditions could never contain the new wine He was introducing.

He was saying that a fixed gulf exists between vital Christianity and the old forms of Judaism. The Judaism of the Old Testament, with its appointed Mosaic order, had indeed mothered Christianity. But just as the child progresses to maturity and independence, so the Christian faith and the Christian evangel were independent of Judaism. Even if Judaism should cease to exist, Christianity as a revelation from God would—and does—stand firmly upon its own solid foundation. It rests upon the same living, speaking God that Judaism rested on.

It is important for us to understand that God, being one in His nature, is always able to say the same thing to everyone who hears Him. He does not have two different messages about grace or love or justice or holiness. Whether it be from the Father or the Son or the Holy Spirit, the revelation will always be the same.

It points in the same direction, though using different ways and different means and different persons.

Begin in Genesis and continue through the Old and New Testaments and you will perceive the uniformity. Yet there are ever-widening elements in God's revelation to mankind. In early Genesis, the Lord spoke in terms of a coming Messiah, foretelling a warfare between the serpent and the Seed of the woman. He noted the victorious Champion-Redeemer who was to come.

The Lord told Eve in very plain words of future human pain in childbearing and of woman's status in the family. He told Adam of the curse upon the ground and of inevitable death as the result of transgression. To Abel and to Cain, He revealed a system of sacrifice and through it a plan of forgiveness and acceptance.

God's message to Noah was of grace and of the order of nature and government. To Abraham, He gave the promise of the coming Seed, the Redeemer who would make atonement for the race. To Moses, He gave the Law and told of the coming Prophet who was to be like Moses and yet superior to him. Those were God's spoken messages "in the past."

GOD'S MESSAGE TO US

Now, what is God saying to His human creation in our day and time? In brief, He is saying, "Jesus Christ is My beloved Son. Hear Him!"

The reason many do not want to hear what God is saying through Jesus to our generation is not hard to guess. God's message in Jesus is a moral pronouncement. It brings to light such elements as faith and conscience and conduct, obedience and loyalty. Men and women reject this message for the same reason they have rejected all of the Bible. They do not wish to be under the authority of the moral Word of God.

For centuries God spoke in many ways. He inspired holy men to write portions of the message in a Book. People do not like it and try their best to avoid it because God has made it the final test of all morality, the final test of all Christian ethics. Some are taking issue with the New Testament record. "How can you prove that Jesus actually said that?" they challenge. Perhaps they are taking issue because they have come across the unforgettable words of Jesus in John's Gospel:

> And if any man hear my words, and believe not, I judge him not: for I came not to judge the world, but to save the world. He that rejecteth me, and receiveth not my words, hath one that judgeth him: the word that I have spoken, the same shall judge him in the last day. (John 12:47–48)

God is a living God and Jesus Christ, with all power and all authority, is at the control panel, guiding and sustaining all things in the universe. That concept is fundamental to the Christian faith. It is necessary that we really and fully comprehend that our God is indeed the Majesty in the heavens.

We can get this assurance from Hebrews, read in the context of the total inspired record. And as we are assured of this, we will have discovered a fundamental means of retaining our sanity in a troubled world and in a selfish society.

If we are going to keep our minds restful at all, we will actually think God into His world—not dismiss Him from His world, as many are trying to do. We will allow Him by faith to be in our beings what He actually is in His world.

The idea that God exists and that He is sovereign in the heavens is absolutely fundamental to human morality. Our view of human decency is also involved in this. Decency is that quality that is proper or becoming. Human decency depends upon an adequate and wholesome concept of God.

Those who take the position that there is no God cannot possibly hold a right and proper view of human nature. That is evident in God's revelation. There is not a man or woman anywhere who can hold an adequate view of our human nature until he or she accepts the fact that we came from God and that we shall return to God again.

We who have admitted Jesus Christ into our lives as Savior and Lord are happy indeed that we did so. In matters of health care, we are familiar with the custom of a "second opinion." If I go to a doctor and he or she advises me to have surgery, I can leave that office and consult with another specialist about my condition. Concerning our decision to receive Jesus Christ, we surely would have been ill-advised to go out and try to get a second opinion! Jesus Christ is God's last word to us. There is no other. God has headed up all of our help and forgiveness and blessing in the person of Jesus Christ, the Son.

In our dark day, God has given us Jesus as the Light of the world. Those who refuse Him give themselves over to the outer darkness that will prevail throughout the eternal ages.

We may not like what the Great Physician tells us about ourselves and our sin. But where else can we go? Peter supplied the answer to that question. "Lord," he said, "to whom shall we go? thou hast the words of eternal life. And we believe and are sure that thou art that Christ, the Son of the living God" (see John 6:68–69).

This is the Savior whom God is offering. He is the eternal Son, equal to the Father in His Godhead, co-eternal and of one substance with the Father.

He is speaking. We should listen!

REFLECT

1. How is it that divine revelation, whether from the Father, the Son, or the Holy Spirit, is always the same?

2. What is the essence of God's message in Jesus?

3. Are there any ways in which you have tried to get a "second opinion" about Jesus or His message?

THE MYSTERY OF THE INCARNATION

*The Word became flesh
and made his dwelling among us.*

John 1:14

We are told that the Word was made flesh. May I point out that within the statement of these few simple words is one of the deepest mysteries of human thought.

Thoughtful men are quick to ask: "How could the deity cross the wide, yawning gulf that separates what is God from that which is not God?" Perhaps you confess with me that in the universe there are really only two things, God and not God—that which is God and that which is not God.

No one could have made God, but God, the Creator, has made all of those things in the universe that are not God.

So, the gulf that separates the Creator and the creature, the gulf between the Being we call God and all other beings, is a great and vast and yawning gulf.

BRIDGING THE GULF

How God could bridge this great gulf is indeed one of the most profound and darkest mysteries to which human thought can be directed.

How is it possible that God could join the Creator to the creature?

If you do not engage in deep thinking, it may not seem so amazing, but if you have given yourself to frequent thoughtful consideration, you are astonished at the bridging of the great gulf between God and not God.

Let us be reminded that the very archangels and the seraphim and the cherubim who shield the stones of fire are not God.

We read our Bibles and discover that man is not the only order of beings. Man in his sinful pride, however, chooses to believe that he is the only such order.

Some Christian people and mankind in general foolishly refuse to believe in the reality of angelic beings. I have talked with enough people to have the feeling that they think of angels as Santa Clauses with wings!

Many say they do not believe in created orders of cherubim and seraphim or watchers or holy ones, or in any of the strange principalities and powers that walk so mysteriously and brightly through the passages of the Bible. Generally speaking, we do not believe in them as much as we should, at any rate.

We may not believe in them, brethren, but they are there!

Mankind is only one order of God's beings or creatures. So, we wonder: "How could the Infinite ever become finite? And how could the Limitless One deliberately impose limitations upon Himself? Why should God favor one order of beings above another in His revelation?"

In the book of Hebrews we learn to our amazement that God took not upon Him the nature of angels, but He took upon Him the seed of Abraham.

Now, Abraham certainly was not equal to an angel.

We would suppose that God, in stepping down, would step down just as little as possible. We would think that He would stop with the angels or the seraphim—but instead He came down to the lowest order and took upon Himself the nature of Abraham, the seed of Abraham.

The apostle Paul throws up his hands in wonder at this point. Paul, declared to be one of the six great intellects of all time, throws up his hands and declares that "great is the mystery of godliness" (1 Tim. 3:16), the mystery of God manifest in the flesh.

Perhaps this is the most becoming approach to the subject for all of us: to just throw up our hands and say, "O Lord, You alone know!" There are so many more things in heaven and earth than are known in our theology—so it is in the deepest sense all mystery.

I would like to quote the gist of what John Wesley said concerning the eternal, mysterious act of God in stooping down to tabernacle with men.

Wesley declared that we should distinguish the act from the method by which the act is performed and advised that we do not reject a fact because we do not know how it was done. I think that is very wise!

I think also that it is very becoming for us to enter into the presence of God reverently, bowing our heads and singing His praises, and acknowledging His loving acts on our behalf even with our words, "It is true, O God, even if we do not know or understand how You have brought it all to pass!"

We will not reject the fact because we do not know the operation that brought it into being.

NO COMPROMISE

How much, then, can we know of this great mystery?

We can surely know this, at least: that the incarnation required no compromise of deity. Let us always remember that when God became incarnate there was no compromise on God's part.

In times past, the mythical gods of the nations were no strangers to compromise. The Roman gods, the gods of the Grecian and Scandinavian legends, were gods that could easily compromise themselves and often did in the tales of mythical lore.

But the holy God who is God, and all else not God, our Father who art in heaven, could never compromise Himself. The incarnation, the Word made flesh, was accomplished without any compromise of the Holy Deity.

The living God did not degrade Himself by this condescension. He did not in any sense make Himself to be less than God.

He remained ever God and everything else remained not God. The gulf still existed even after Jesus Christ had become man and had dwelt among us. Instead of God degrading Himself when He became man, by the act of incarnation He elevated mankind to Himself.

It is plain in the Athanasian Creed that the early church fathers were cautious at this point of doctrine. They would not allow us to believe that God, in the incarnation, became flesh by a coming down of the Deity into flesh; but rather by the taking up of mankind into God.

Thus, we do not degrade God but we elevate man—and that is the wonder of redemption!

Then, too, there is another thing that we can know for sure about the acts of God—and that is that God can never back out of His bargain. This union of man with God is effected unto perpetuity!

In the sense that we have been considering, God can never cease to be man, for the second Person of the Trinity can never un-incarnate Himself, or de-incarnate Himself. The incarnation remains forever a fact, for "the Word was made flesh, and dwelt among us" (John 1:14).

We ought to turn our thoughts here to those earlier days in man's history, for after God had created Adam we know that the Creator communed with men.

I have leafed through a book titled *Earth's Earliest Ages*. I will not say that I have actually read it because I quickly concluded that the author seems to believe that he knows more about the antediluvian period than Moses did. When I discover a man who claims to know more than Moses on a subject in which Moses is a specialist, I shy away from his book.

I admit that I like to dream and dwell in my thoughts upon those ages long past. I have always been fascinated by the Genesis passage that tells us that God came and walked in the garden in the cool of the day, calling for Adam. But Adam was not there.

I do not think we are reading anything into the account by assuming that God's meeting with Adam in this way was a common custom at that time. We are not told that this was the first time that God had come to take a walk with Adam in the midst of birdsong and in the fading light.

God and man walked together and because the Creator had made man in His own image there was no degradation in His communion with man.

But now Adam is in hiding. Pride and disobedience, doubt and failure in testing—sin has broken off the communion and fellowship of the Creator with the created. The holy God must reject the fallen man, sending him from the garden and setting up a flaming sword that he might not return.

THE LOST PRESENCE

Adam had lost the presence of the Creator God and in the Bible record of the ages that followed, God never dwelt with men again in quite the same way.

To the Israelites, God dwelt in the Shekinah, hidden in the fire and the cloud. Occasionally He would appear in what theologians call a theophany, an appearance of the Deity. God might speak briefly with a man as He did with Abraham in the tent door or with Gideon on the threshing floor. God did not linger; His appearance always cautious and veiled.

Even when God showed Himself to Moses it was in the fire of the burning bush or while Moses was hidden in the cleft of the rock. The eyes of fallen, sinful men were no longer able to endure the radiant majesty and glory of deity.

Then, in the fullness of time, He came again to men, for "the Word was made flesh, and dwelt among us."

They called His name "Immanuel," which means "God with us." In that first coming of Jesus the Christ, God again came to dwell with men in person.

I will have you know that I am not a prepositional preacher but at this point we must note three prepositions having to do with the coming of Jesus, God appearing as man.

He appeared to dwell with men. He appeared to be united to men. He came to ultimately dwell in men forever. So, it is with men, and to men and in men that He came to dwell.

I always note with a little chuckle the frustrations of the translators when they come to such passages as "No man hath seen God at any time, the only begotten Son, which is in the bosom of the Father, he hath declared him" (John 1:18).

God's Word is just too big for the translators. They come to this phrase in the Greek: "The Son hath declared Him." In the English of the King James Version it is just "declared." In other versions they skirt it, they go around it, they plunge through it. They use two or three words and then they come back to one. They do everything to try to say what the Holy Ghost said, but they have to give up. Our English just will not say it all.

When we have used up our words and synonyms, we still have not said all that God revealed when He said: Nobody has ever seen God, but when Jesus Christ came He showed us what God is like (paraphrase of John 1:18).

I suppose that our simple and everyday language is as good as any.

He has revealed Him—He has shown us what God is like!

He has declared Him. He has set Him forth. He has revealed

Him. In these ways the translators shift their language trying to get at this wondrous miracle of meaning.

But that man walking in Galilee was God acting like God. It was God, limited deliberately, having crossed the wide, mysterious gulf between God and not God; God and creature. No man had seen God at any time.

"The only begotten Son, which is in the bosom of the Father . . ." (John 1:18)—will you note that *was* is not the tense? Neither does it say that the Son *will be* in the Father's bosom. He *is* in the Father's bosom. It is stated in present, perpetual tense; the continuous tense, I think the grammarians call it. It is the language of continuation.

Therefore, when Jesus hung on the cross He did not leave the bosom of the Father.

You ask me, then: "Mr. Tozer, if that is true, why did our Lord Jesus cry out, 'My God, my God, why hast thou forsaken me?'" (Mark 15:34).

Was He frightened? Was He mistaken?

Never, never!

The answer should be very plain to us who love Him and serve Him.

Even when Christ Jesus died on that unholy, fly-infested cross for mankind, He never divided the Godhead. As the old theologians pointed out, you cannot divide the substance. Not all of Nero's swords could ever cut down through the substance of the Godhead to cut off the Father from the Son.

It was Mary's son who cried out, "Why hast thou forsaken me?"

It was the human body that God had given Him.

It was the sacrifice that cried, the lamb about to die.

It was the human Jesus. It was the Son of Man who cried.

Believe it that the ancient and timeless Deity was never separated; He was still in the bosom of the Father when He cried, "Into thy hands I commend my spirit" (Luke 23:46).

So the cross did not divide the Godhead—nothing can ever do that. One forever, indivisible, the substance undivided, three persons unconfounded.

Oh, the wonder of the ancient theology of the Christian church! How little we know of it in our day of light-minded shallowness. How much we ought to know of it.

"No man hath seen God at any time, the only begotten Son, which is in the bosom of the Father, he hath declared him" (John 1:18).

REFLECT

1. How is the incarnation of God the Son different from the legends of Roman, Greek, and Scandinavian gods?

2. What happened to humanity when God became man?

3. When God the Son became man and suffered on the cross, was the Godhead divided? Why or why not?

THE CENTER OF ALL

. . . Christ is all, and is in all.

COLOSSIANS 3:11

Christ is the center of all things. He is, as it were, the hub of a wheel around which everything revolves. Centuries ago someone said that Christ is like the hub and everything that has been created is on the rim of the wheel.

One of the old church fathers said, "Everything that exists is equally distant from Jesus and equally near to Him."

There is the hub in the middle of each wheel with spokes going out to the rim. Then, in the perfectly shaped wheel, the rim goes around equal distance at all points from the hub. To us, Jesus Christ is that hub and everything else is on the rim. When Jesus Christ has His place as hub, we are all equally close or equally far from Him.

Jesus is in the midst, and because that is true, He is accessible from anywhere in life. This is good news—wonderful, good news!

This truth makes it possible for us to insist that Jesus Christ is at the center of geography. No one, therefore, can claim an advantage with Christ because of location.

CENTER OF GEOGRAPHY

It so happens that I am at the present time reading *History of Latin Christianity* and have read again the story of the Crusaders. At the time of the historic crusade, many believed that merit was to be gained by making a pilgrimage to the very place where Jesus was born, and particularly to the sepulcher where His body was laid.

When Peter the Hermit, old and barefooted, whipped all of Europe into a white heat to get the crusades launched, he set the goal of liberating a grave out of which Jesus Christ had stepped more than a thousand years before. The Crusaders felt that if that empty tomb could be taken from the Muslims, everything would be all right. Today there is still great interest in being where Jesus had been, but I don't know why we insist upon being spiritually obtuse.

Have we not heard Jesus' words: "I tell you that neither in this mountain nor in Jerusalem do men worship the Father, for the Father seeketh such to worship Him who worship Him in spirit and in truth" (see John 4:21–24). It is not on a certain mountain or in a city!

We wonder why the Crusaders did not consider that. Why all the bloody wounds, starvation, suffering, and death? Why the long, weary treks to get to the place where Jesus had been born or where He died, or where He had been buried? For there is no geographical advantage anywhere in the world. Not one of us would be a better Christian just by living in Jerusalem. If you lived at some spot in the world actually farther from Jerusalem, you would be at no disadvantage. Jesus Christ is in the very center of geography. It is just as near to Him from anywhere as it is from anywhere else! And it's just as far from Him also! So geography doesn't mean anything in our relationship to Him!

Plenty of money has been spent by preachers who felt that they could preach better if they could just visit Jerusalem. So they go over and look on Jerusalem, and when they come back, they have just a few more stories to tell. Actually, they are no better and their audiences are no better. Let's believe it—Jesus is the hub and geography is all around Him!

CENTER OF TIME

Then, we must come to the conclusion that Jesus Christ is the center of time. Many people become sad when they talk about missing the time of Christ on earth. It is good to recall and study the life and ministries of Jesus long ago. We sing a song that says:

I think when I read that sweet story of old,
When Jesus was here among men,
How He called little children as lambs to His fold,
I should like to have been with Him then!

Many a tear has been wiped out of the eyes when people have sung that, but did you know that the people who were with Jesus at the time when He walked among men were not as well off as they were ten days after He left them?

Ten days after He departed, He sent the Holy Spirit, and the disciples who understood only in part suddenly knew the plan of God as in a blaze of light.

But we say, "I would like to have lived in the time of Christ."

Why? There were hypocrites and Pharisees and opposers, murderers, and unbelievers in the time of Christ! You would not have found things any better two thousand years ago.

Some of you who look back with nostalgia upon what you consider the good old days ought to be delivered from that!

CENTER OF HUMANITY

Consider, too, that Jesus Christ is the center of the human race. With Him there are no favored races. We had better come to the point of believing that Jesus Christ is the Son of Man. He is not the Son of the first century nor the twentieth century. He is the Son of Man—not a Son of the Jewish race only. He is the Son of all races no matter what the color or tongue.

When Jesus Christ was incarnated in mortal flesh, He was not incarnated only in the body of the Jew, but in the body of the whole human race.

Go to Tibet or Afghanistan, to the Indians of South America, the Mohammedans of Arabia, the Englishmen of London, or the Scots of Glasgow and preach Jesus. If there is faith and willingness to follow, He will bring them all into His fellowship. They are all in the rim. They are all as near and all as far. That's the reason for the kind of missionary philosophy we hold. We do not first go into a country to educate the people and then preach Christ to them. We know better than that! We know that Jesus Christ is just as near to an uneducated, uncultured native as He is to a polished gentleman from New York or London. Christ is at the center of all cultural levels. Preach Christ and show the love of God to the most primitive, most neglected, most illiterate people in the world; be patient and make them understand. Their hearts will awake, the Spirit will illuminate their minds. Those who believe on Jesus will be transformed. This is a beautiful thing that is being demonstrated over and over again in the world today.

In New Guinea and throughout parts of Indonesia, for instance, stone-age men and repulsive cannibals are being born again just as quickly as those with college degrees, because it is just as near to Jesus from the jungle as it is from the halls of ivy.

He is in the midst of all cultures!

Jesus is in the midst of all ages as well. By that I mean our human ages, our birthdays. It is just as near to Jesus at eighty years old as it is from eight; just as near from seventy as it is from seven.

We have been told that as we get older, we are harder to reach for God and the likelihood of our coming to Jesus diminishes. But our ability to come to Jesus—the distance we are from God—is no greater when we are ninety than when we were youngsters.

So, Jesus Christ stands in the middle of the human race, at the center of geography, the central figure in time, and in the midst of all cultures.

Our Lord is at the center of all life's experiences!

ANYONE CAN REACH HIM

Our Lord speaks peace to us throughout life's experiences. An experience is awareness of things taking place around us. A newborn baby does not have experience. So far, he is just a little stranger in our world. But he learns fast, and very soon experience will teach him that when he howls, he will get attention.

The man who lives to be one hundred years old has really had some experiences. However, if he lives somewhere in the hills and seldom comes out, he probably will have a narrow field of experience.

If he is a world traveler with a good education and a wide circle of friends, his experience will be so vast that it is a mystery as to how his brain can file away so much for future memory and reference.

I ask, which is nearer to Jesus? Does the child with little experience have an advantage over the man of wide experience? There is no difference! Jesus Christ stands in the middle of life's experiences and anyone can reach Him, no matter who he is!

Jonathan Edwards, that mighty preacher of the earlier days in our country, was converted when he was only five years old. He wrote, "I never backslid. I went right on." What experiences can a five-year-old boy have?

Read the early chapters of 1 Samuel and consider that the boy Samuel was twelve. He was just a lad. And then there was Eli, ninety-eight years old. Here are the two of them—the boy and the aged man.

What experience had the boy had? Practically none. What experience had the old man had? Practically all. He had run the whole scale, the gamut of human possibilities. Yet it was just as near to God from young Samuel who had no experience as it was to Eli who had found out through the years what life was all about.

Remember that when our Lord hung on the cross, a superscription was written in Hebrew, Greek, and Latin and placed on the cross above His head: "This is Jesus Christ, the King of the Jews." Someone has pointed out that in doing this, God had taken in the whole world. Hebrew stands for religion; Greek for philosophy, and Latin for Rome's military prowess. All the possibilities of human experience on a world scale were taken in.

It was just as close from the Roman soldiers to the Son of God as from the Hebrew teacher, Nicodemus, who said, "Master, Thou art sent from God!"

So, the world of that day was really divided into three parts, and that is about all we have today, isn't it?

We still have religion, culture, and the combination of military and politics. Everything else seems to fall somewhere inside those brackets.

Jesus Christ was crucified in the very center of man's world. So it is just as easy to reach Him from the philosopher's ivory tower as it is from the priest's sanctuary. It is just as easy for the uniformed soldier to reach Him as it is for the thinker with his big books.

Christ Jesus our Lord stands in the midst so no one can claim advantage. Thank God! No one can frighten me, intimidate me, or send me away.

No one can put me down and say, "Ah, but you don't know!"

They have tried. They smile when they say it and I smile back and think, "Brother, you are the one who doesn't know—because I do know!"

I know that I can reach Him as quickly from where I am as any other man.

63

Einstein, with his great mind, could reach out and touch his Messiah if he would. There are many in America who cannot read or write. Einstein and the man who marks an *X* for his name are in the same category. Both are equal on the rim. No man can actually say that he has been given an advantage over others.

You say, then: "Why doesn't everybody come?"

Because of inexcusable stubbornness.

Because of unbelief.

Because of preoccupation with other things.

Because we do not believe that we really need Him!

Millions turn their backs on Him because they will not confess their need. If you have found you need Him, you can come to Him in faith, you can touch Him and feel His power flowing out to help you, whoever you are.

Jesus did not come to save learned men only. He came to save the sinner! Not white men only—but all colors that are under the sun. Not young people only—but people of all ages!

Let us believe that and let us honor Jesus in our midst! The most important thing about you and Jesus is that you can reach Him from where you are!

REFLECT

1. How is it that Jesus is the center of all things? How does this knowledge impact your life?

2. Why do you think it is so difficult to reach out for the help of Christ in everyday life?

7

MIRACLE WORKER

*. . . how God anointed Jesus of Nazareth with the
Holy Spirit and power, and how he went around
doing good and healing all who were under the
power of the devil, because God was with him.*

ACTS 10:38

If we have the anointing of the Holy Spirit and His presence in
our lives, we should be able to do what Jesus, the Son of Man,
was able to do in His earthly ministry.

Please do not close this book and turn away when I tell you
of my persuasion. I am persuaded that our Lord Jesus, while
He was on earth, did not accomplish His powerful deeds in the
strength of His deity. I believe He did them in the strength and
authority of His Spirit-anointed humanity.

My reasoning is this: If Jesus had come to earth and performed His ministry in the power of His deity, what He did
would have been accepted as a matter of course. Cannot God do
anything He wants to do? No one would have questioned His

works as the works of deity. But Jesus veiled His deity and minis-
tered as a man. It is noteworthy, however, that He did not begin
His ministry—His deeds of authority and power—until He had
been anointed with the Holy Spirit.

I know there are erudite scholars and theological experts
who will dispute my conclusion. Nevertheless, I hold it true.
Jesus Christ, in the power and authority of His Spirit-anointed
humanity, stilled the waves, quieted the winds, healed the
sick, gave sight to the blind, exercised complete authority over
demons, and raised the dead. He did all the miraculous things
He was moved to do among men not as God, which would not
have been miraculous at all, but as a Spirit-anointed man. Re-
markable! . . .

Review with me the message of the apostle Peter to Cornelius
and his Gentile household:

How God anointed Jesus of Nazareth with the Holy Ghost
and with power: who went about doing good, and healing
all that were oppressed of the devil; for God was with him.
(Acts 10:38)

The letter to the Hebrews says the anointing God placed
upon Jesus was an anointing above His fellows. It is my feeling
that the "anointing above His fellows" was not given because
God chose to so anoint Him, but because He was willing. He
could be anointed to that extent!

What did the anointing signify?

Going back into the Levitical priesthood, we discover a ritual
of an anointing with a specially prepared holy oil. Certain pun-

gent herbs were beaten into the oil, making it fragrant and aromatic. It was unique; Israel could not use that formula for any other oil. When a priest was set apart and anointed, the oil was a vivid type of the New Testament anointing of the Holy Spirit. The holy anointing oil could only be used for the anointing of men with special ministries—priests, as I have indicated, and kings and prophets. It was not intended for the carnal, sinful person.

In Leviticus we read of the consecration of Aaron as the first high priest. The anointing oil and the blood from the altar are mentioned together: "And Moses took of the anointing oil, and of the blood which was upon the altar, and sprinkled it upon Aaron, and upon his garments . . . and sanctified Aaron, and his garments" (8:30).

The fragrance of the anointing oil was unique. If someone went near an Old Testament priest, he could say immediately, "I smell an anointed man. I smell the holy oil!" The aroma, the pungency, the fragrance were there. Such an anointing could not be kept a secret.

In the New Testament, when the Holy Spirit came, His presence fulfilled that whole list of fragrances found in the holy anointing oil. When New Testament believers were anointed, that anointing was evident. Read it in the book of Acts:

And they were all filled with the Holy Ghost. (2:4)

They were all filled with the Holy Ghost, and they spake the word of God with boldness. (4:31)

But he [Stephen], being full of the Holy Ghost, looked up stedfastly into heaven. (7:55)

While Peter yet spake these words, the Holy Ghost fell on all them which heard the word. (10:44)

The list goes on.

The Holy Spirit has not changed. His power and authority have not changed. He is still the third Person of the eternal Godhead. He is among us to teach us all we need to know about Jesus Christ, the eternal Son of God.

THE ANOINTING IS NO SECRET

I am suggesting—indeed, I am stating—that no one among us, man or woman, can be genuinely anointed with the Holy Spirit and hope to keep it a secret. His or her anointing will be evident.

A Christian brother once confided in me how he had tried to keep the fullness of the Spirit a secret within his own life. He had made a commitment of his life to God in faith. In answer to prayer, God had filled him with the Spirit. Within himself he said, "I cannot tell anyone about this!"

Three days passed. On the third day his wife touched him on the arm and asked, "Everett, what has happened to you? Something has happened to you!" And like a pent-up stream his testimony flowed out. He had received an anointing of the Holy Spirit. The fragrance could not be hidden. His wife knew it in the home. His life was changed. The spiritual graces and fruits of the consecrated life cannot be hidden. It is an anointing with the oil of gladness and joy.

I am happy to tell everyone that the power of the Spirit is glad power! Our Savior, Jesus Christ, lived His beautiful, holy life on earth and did His healing, saving deeds of power in the strength of this oil of gladness.

We must admit that there was more of the holy oil of God on the head of Jesus than on your head or mine—or on the head of anyone else who has ever lived. That is not to say that God will withhold His best from anyone. But the Spirit of God can only anoint in proportion to the willingness He finds in our lives. In the case of Jesus, we are told that He had a special anointing because He loved righteousness and hated iniquity. That surely gives us the clue we need concerning the kind of persons we must be in order to receive the full anointing and blessing from Almighty God.

When Jesus was on earth, He was not the passive, colorless, spineless person He is sometimes made out to be in paintings and literature. He was a strong man, a man of iron will. He was able to love with an intensity of love that burned Him up. He was able to hate with the strongest degree of hatred against everything that was wrong and evil and selfish and sinful.

Invariably someone will object when I make a statement like that. "I cannot believe such things about Jesus. I always thought it was a sin to hate!"

Study long and well the record and the teachings of Jesus while He was on earth. In them lies the answer. It is a sin for the children of God not to hate what ought to be hated. Our Lord Jesus loved righteousness, but He hated iniquity. I think we can say He hated sin and wrong and evil perfectly!

If we are committed, consecrated Christians, truly disciples of the crucified and risen Christ, there are some things we must face.

We cannot love honesty without hating dishonesty.

We cannot love purity without hating impurity.

We cannot love truth without hating lying and deceitfulness.

If we belong to Jesus Christ, we must hate evil even as He hated evil in every form. The ability of Jesus Christ to hate that which was against God and to love that which was full of God was the force that made Him able to receive the anointing—the oil of gladness—in complete measure. On our human side, it is our imperfection in loving the good and hating the evil that prevents us from receiving the Holy Spirit in complete measure. God withholds from us because we are unwilling to follow Jesus in His great poured-out love for what is right and His pure and holy hatred of what is evil.

REFLECT

1. Why is it significant that Jesus, as a man, performed miracles by the power of the Holy Spirit and not just by His own divine power?

2. How does the New Testament depiction of Jesus differ from the way He is often portrayed in our world today?

3. How different would your life look if you received a fuller measure of the Holy Spirit?

8

THE PEOPLE'S SAVIOR

*For God did not send his Son into the world to
condemn the world, but to save the world through him.*

JOHN 3:17

Now, when the Word says that God sent His Son into the world, it is not talking to us merely about the world as geography. It does not just indicate to us that God sent His Son into the Near East, that He sent Him to Bethlehem in Palestine.

He came to Bethlehem, certainly. He did come to that little land that lies between the seas. But this message does not have any geographical or astronomical meaning. It has nothing to do with kilometers and distances and continents and mountains and towns.

What it really means is that God sent His Son into the human race. When it speaks of the world here, it does not mean that God just loved our geography. It does not mean that God so

71

loved the snow-capped mountains or the sun-kissed meadows or the flowing streams or the great peaks of the north.

God may love all of these. I think He does. You cannot read the book of Job or the Psalms without knowing that God is in love with the world He made.

But that is not the meaning in this passage. God sent His Son to the human race. He came to people. This is something we must never forget—Jesus Christ came to seek and to save people. Not just certain favored people. Not just certain kinds of people. Not just people in general.

We humans do have a tendency to use generic terms and general terms and pretty soon we become just scientific in our outlook. Let us cast that outlook aside and confess that God loved each of us in a special kind of way so that His Son came into and unto and upon the people of the world—and He even became one of those people!

If you could imagine yourself to be like Puck* and able to draw a ring around the earth in forty winks, just think of the kinds of people you would see all at once. You would see the crippled and the blind and the leprous. You would see the fat, the lean, the tall, and the short. You would see the dirty and the clean. You would see some walking safely along the avenues with no fear of a policeman but you would see also those who skulk in back alleys and crawl through broken windows. You would see those who are healthy and you would see others twitching and twisting in the last agonies of death. You would see the ignorant and the illiterate as well as those gathered under the elms

Note
* Puck is a character in William Shakespeare's *A Midsummer Night's Dream.*

in some college town, nurturing deep dreams of great poems or plays or books to astonish and delight the world.

People! You would see the millions of people: people whose eyes slant differently from yours and people whose hair is not like your hair. Their customs are not the same as yours, their habits are not the same. But they are all people. The thing is, their differences are all external. Their similarities are all within their natures. Their differences have to do with customs and habits. Their likeness has to do with nature.

HE CAME FOR ALL PEOPLE

Brethren, let us treasure this: God sent His Son to the people. He is the people's Savior. Jesus Christ came to give life and hope to people like your family and like mine.

The Savior of the world knows the true value and worth of every living soul. He pays no attention to status or human honor or class. Our Lord knows nothing about this status business that everyone talks about.

When Jesus came to this world, He never asked anyone, "What is your IQ?" He never asked anyone whether or not they were well-traveled. Let us thank God that He sent Him—and that He came! Both of those things are true. They are not contradictory. God sent Him as Savior! Christ, the Son, came to seek and to save! He came because He was sent and He came because His great heart urged Him and compelled Him to come. Now, let's think about the mission on which He came. Do you know what I have been thinking about our situation as people, as humans?

Let us think and imagine ourselves back to the condition of paganism. Let us imagine that we have no Bible and no hymn book and that these two thousand years of Christian teaching and tradition had never taken place. We are on our own, humanly speaking.

Suddenly, someone arrives with a proclamation: "God is sending His Son into the human race. He is coming!"

What would be the first thing that we would think of? What would our hearts and consciences tell us immediately? We would run for the trees and rocks and hide like Adam among the trees of the garden.

What would be the logical mission upon which God would send His Son into the world? We know what our nature is and we know that God knows all about us and He is sending His Son to face us.

Why would the Son of God come to our race?

Our own hearts—sin and darkness and deception and moral disease tell us what His mission should be. The sin we cannot deny tells us that He might have come to judge the world!

Why did the Holy Ghost bring this proclamation and word from God that "God sent not his Son into the world to condemn the world" (John 3:17)?

Men and women are condemned in their own hearts because they know that if the Righteous One is coming, then we ought to be sentenced.

But God had a greater and far more gracious purpose—He came that sinful men might be saved. The loving mission of our Lord Jesus Christ was not to condemn but to forgive and reclaim.

Why did He come to men and not to fallen angels? Well, I believe He came to men and not to angels because man at the first was created in the image of God and angels were not. I believe He came to fallen Adam's brood and not to fallen devils because the fallen brood of Adam had once borne the very image of God.

Thus, I believe it was a morally logical decision, that when Jesus Christ became incarnate it was in the flesh and body of a man because God had made man in His image.

I believe that although man was fallen and lost and on his way to hell, he still had a capacity and potential that made the incarnation possible, so that God Almighty could pull up the blankets of human flesh around His ears and become a Man to walk among men.

There was nothing of like kind among angels and fallen creatures—so He came not to condemn but to reclaim and to restore and to regenerate.

We have been trying to think of this condescension of God in personal and individual terms and what it should mean to each one of us to be loved of God in this way.

Now I think I hear someone saying, "But John 3:16 does not mention the cross. You have been telling about God's love but you have not mentioned the cross and His death on our behalf!"

Just let me say that there are some who insist and imagine that whenever we preach we should just open our mouths and in one great big round paragraph include every bit of theology there is to preach.

John 3:16 does not mention the cross and I declare to you that God is not nearly as provincial as we humans are. He has revealed it all and has included it all and has said it all somewhere in the Book, so that the cross stands out like a great, bright, shining pillar in the midst of the Scriptures.

We remember, too, that without the cross on which the Savior died there could be no Scriptures, no revelation, no redemptive message, nothing! But here He gave us a loving proclamation— He sent His Son; He gave His Son! Then later it develops that in giving His Son, He gave Him to die!

I have said that this must be a personal word for every man and every woman. Like a prodigal son in that most moving of all stories, each one of us must come to grips with our own personal need and to decide and act as he did: "I perish with hunger. I will arise and go to my father" (Luke 15:17–18). He said, "I will arise"—so he got up and went to his father.

You must think of yourself—for God sent His Son into the world to save you!

Here I insist that you must have some faith about yourself and I am almost afraid to say it because someone will send me a critical, nagging letter.

I am not asking you to have faith in yourself—I am only insisting that it is right for you to show faith about yourself, faith in Christ and in what He has promised you as an individual person.

That is, you must believe that you are the one He meant when He said, "Come home."

HE MEANT YOU AND ME

All of the general faith you have about God will not do you any good at all unless you are willing to believe that He meant you—you yourself—when He said, "God so loves that He gave His Son for you!"

The prodigal son could have said in general terms: "When one is hungry and ready to perish, one could return to his father's house." But he said, "I am the one that is hungry. I am the one for whom my father has a complete provision. I will arise and go!"

God lovingly waits for each individual to come with a personal resolve and decision: "I will arise and I will go home to claim the provision in my Father's house." If you will make that personal decision of faith in Jesus Christ, with faith in the fact that it is really you whom God loves and wants to forgive, it will mean something more to you than you have ever known—something beautiful and eternal.

I close by reminding you also as an individual that unbelief always finds three trees behind which to hesitate and hide. Here they are: Somebody Else. Some Other Place. Some Other Time.

We hear someone preaching an invitation sermon on John 3:16 and in effect we run to the garden to hide behind these trees.

"Of course it is true," we say, "but it is for Somebody Else."

If it were only Some Other Place or at Some Other Time you might be willing to come.

Whether you get the right grammar or the proper tense is not important: what our Lord is delighted to hear is your confession that "that means me, Lord! I am the reason, the cause and reason why You came to earth to die."

That is positive, personal faith in a personal Redeemer—and that is what saves you. I give you my word that if you will just rush in there, just as you are and with faith in Jesus Christ, our Lord has very little concern as to whether or not you know all of the theology in the world!

REFLECT

1. Does the knowledge that God sent His Son to save *all* people give you boldness, or do you struggle to accept that as true?

2. Why do you think many non-Christians see God as a vindictive bully out to punish people?

9

THE REMEDY

Peace be with you!

John 20:21

Contrary to the opinion held by many would-be religious leaders in the world, Christianity was never intended to be an "ethical system" with Jesus Christ at the head.

Our Lord did not come into the world two thousand years ago to launch Christianity as a new religion or a new system. He came into this world with eternal purpose. He came as the center of all things. Actually, He came to be our religion, if you wish to put it that way.

He came in person, in the flesh, to be God's salvation to the very ends of the earth. He did not come just to delegate power to others to heal or cure or bless. He came to *be* the blessing, for all the blessings and the full glory of God are to be found in His person. Because Jesus Christ is the center of all things, He offers deliverance for the human soul and mind by His direct, personal, and intimate touch. This is not my one-man interpretation. It is the basic teaching of salvation through the Messiah-Savior, Jesus Christ. It is a teaching that runs throughout the Bible!

I remind you that Jesus Christ came into a world of complex religious observances. Perhaps it can be likened to a kind of religious jungle, with a choking and confusing multiplicity of duties, rituals, and observances laid upon the people. It was a jungle grown so thick with man-made ordinances that it brought only a continuing darkness.

Into the midst of all this came the Light that was able to light every man that was to come into the world. He could say and teach, "I am the light of the world," because He shone so brightly, dispelling the darkness.

Jesus Christ came in the fullness of time to be God's salvation. He was to be God's cure for all that was wrong with the human race.

He came to deliver us from our moral and spiritual disorders—but it must also be said He came to deliver us from our own remedies.

OUR REAL CURE

Religion as a form is one of the heaviest burdens that has ever been laid upon the human race, and we must observe that it is a self-medicating burden. Men and women who are conscious of their moral and spiritual disorders try to medicate themselves, hoping to get better by their own treatment.

I often wonder if there is any kind of self-cure or human medication that man has not tried in his efforts to restore himself and gain merit.

Millions of pilgrims may still be seen in India, flat on the ground, crawling like inchworms toward the Ganges River, hoping for a release from the burden of guilt in the sacred waters.

History tells of countless persons who have tried to deal with guilt by self-denial and abstaining from food and drink. Many have tried a kind of self-torture by putting on hair shirts or walking on spikes or on hot coals. Men with the hermit complex have shunned society and hidden themselves in caves, hoping to gain some merit that would bring them closer to God and compensate for their own sinful nature.

Mankind is still inventing new ways of self-treatment and medication for failures and weaknesses and wrongdoing, even in our own day, not recognizing that the cure has already come.

Simeon, the old man of God who had waited in hope around the temple, knew that the cure had come! When he saw the baby Jesus, he took Him up in his arms, looked down at Him, and said, "Lord, now lettest thou thy servant depart in peace . . . for mine eyes have seen thy salvation" (Luke 2:29–30).

So, I say to those who doubt or to those who are not instructed that it is Jesus Christ Himself that Christianity offers to you. I know that some churches are confused because of the introduction of human ideas, such as the self-medication idea, which has grown and expanded much like the proverbial mustard tree.

But, really, all Christianity offers is Jesus Christ the Lord, and Him alone—for He is enough! Your relation to Jesus Christ is really the all-important matter in this life.

That is both good news and bad news. It is good news for

all who have met our Savior and know Him intimately and personally. It is bad news for those who hope to get into heaven some other way!

OUR PEACE

Notice in the record that Jesus stood in the midst and said, "Peace be unto you."

Here is a beautiful explanation of the angels' words, "Peace on earth, good will to men." The angels could say that only because it was Jesus who was coming! He is our peace. I once had a wall motto that said, "He is our peace." Because of the coming of Jesus, the angels could announce, "Peace on earth."

This portion of Scripture illustrated Jesus' method of imparting health, directly and personally. It was Christ in the midst— at the center—and He could take that place because He is God, He is spirit, He is timeless, He is spaceless, He is supreme, He is all in all. Therefore, He could be at the center! . . .

Jesus did not come to save learned men only. He came to save the sinner! Not white men only—but all colors that are under the sun. Not young people only—but people of all ages!

Let us believe that and let us honor Jesus in our midst! The most important thing about you and Jesus is that you can reach Him from where you are.

REFLECT

1. Why is the solution that Christianity offers different than what other religions offer?

2. Do you think non-Christians would respond differently if they grasped that what Christianity offers is simply Jesus?

THE OFFERING

How much more, then, will the blood of Christ,
who through the eternal Spirit offered himself
unblemished to God, cleanse our consciences from acts
that lead to death, so that we may serve the living God!

Hebrews 9:14

The word *passion* now means "sex lust," but back in the early days it meant deep, terrible suffering. That is why they call Good Friday "Passion Tide," and we talk about "the passion of Christ." It is the suffering Jesus did as He made His priestly offering with His own blood for us.

Jesus Christ is God, and all I've said about God describes Christ. He is unitary. He has taken on Himself the nature of man, but God the Eternal Word, who was before man and who created man is a unitary being and there is no dividing of His substance. And so that Holy One suffered, and His suffering in His own blood for us was three things. It was infinite, almighty, and perfect.

Infinite means without bound and without limit, shoreless, bottomless, topless forever and ever, without any possible measure or limitation. And so the suffering of Jesus and the atonement He made on that cross under that darkening sky was infinite in its power.

It was not only infinite but almighty. It's possible for good men to "almost" do something or to "almost" be something. That is the fix people get in because they are people. But Almighty God is never "almost" anything. God is always exactly what He is. He is the Almighty One. Isaac Watts said about His dying on the cross, "God the mighty Maker died for man the creature's sin." And when God the Almighty Maker died, all the power there is was in that atonement. You never can overstate the efficaciousness of the atonement. You never can exaggerate the power of the cross.

And God is not only infinite and almighty, but also perfect. The atonement in Jesus Christ's blood is perfect; there isn't anything that can be added to it. It is spotless, impeccable, flawless. It is perfect as God is perfect. So the question, "How dost Thou spare the wicked if Thou art just?" is answered from the effect of Christ's passion. That holy suffering there on the cross and that resurrection from the dead cancels our sins and abrogates our sentence.

Where and how did we get that sentence? We got it by the application of justice to a moral situation. No matter how nice and refined and lovely you think you are, you are a moral situation—you have been, you still are, you will be. And when God confronted you, God's justice confronted a moral situation and found you unequal—found inequity, found iniquity.

Because He found iniquity there, God sentenced you to die.

Everybody has been or is under the sentence of death. I wonder how people can be so jolly under the sentence of death. "The soul that sinneth, it shall die" (Ezek. 18:20). When justice confronts a moral situation in a man, woman, young person, or anybody morally responsible, then either it justifies or condemns that person. That's how we got that sentence.

Let me point out that when God in His justice sentences the sinner to die, He does not quarrel with the mercy of God; He does not quarrel with the kindness of God; He does not quarrel with His compassion or pity, for they are all attributes of a unitary God, and they cannot quarrel with each other. All the attributes of God concur in a man's death sentence. The very angels in heaven cried out and said, "Thou art righteous, O Lord, which art, and wast, and shalt be, because thou hast judged thus. . . . Even so, Lord God Almighty, true and righteous are thy judgments" (Rev. 16:5,7).

You'll never find in heaven a group of holy beings finding fault with the way God conducts His foreign policy. God Almighty is conducting His world, and every moral creature says, "True and righteous are thy judgments. . . . Justice and judgment are the habitation of thy throne" (Rev. 16:7, Ps. 89:14). When God sends a man to die, mercy and pity and compassion and wisdom and power concur—everything that's intelligent in God concurs in the sentence.

THE REASON CHRIST DIED

But oh, the mystery and wonder of the atonement! The soul that avails itself of that atonement, that throws itself out on that atonement, the moral situation has changed. God has not changed! Jesus Christ did not die to change God; Jesus Christ died to change a moral situation. When God's justice confronts an unprotected sinner that justice sentences him to die. And all of God concurs in the sentence! But when Christ, who is God, went onto the tree and died there in infinite agony, in a plethora of suffering, this great God suffered more than they suffer in hell. He suffered all that they could suffer in hell. He suffered with the agony of God, for everything that God does, He does with all that He is. When God suffered for you, my friend, God suffered to change your moral situation.

The man who throws himself on the mercy of God has had the moral situation changed. God doesn't say, "Well, we'll excuse this fellow. He's made his decision, and we'll forgive him. He's gone into the prayer room, so we'll pardon him. He's going to join the church; we'll overlook his sin." No! When God looks at an atoned-for sinner He doesn't see the same moral situation that He sees when He looks at a sinner who still loves his sin. When God looks at a sinner who still loves his sin and rejects the mystery of the atonement, justice condemns him to die. When God looks at a sinner who has accepted the blood of the everlasting covenant, justice sentences him to live. And God is just in doing both things.

When God justifies a sinner everything in God is on the sinner's side. All the attributes of God are on the sinner's side. It isn't that mercy is pleading for the sinner and justice is trying to beat him to death, as we preachers sometimes make it sound. All of God does all that God does. When God looks at a sinner and sees him there unatoned for (he won't accept the atonement; he thinks it doesn't apply to him), the moral situation is such that justice says he must die. And when God looks at the atoned-for sinner, who in faith knows he's atoned for and has accepted it, justice says he must live! The unjust sinner can no more go to heaven than the justified sinner can go to hell. Oh friends, why are we so still? Why are we so quiet? We ought to rejoice and thank God with all our might!

I say it again: Justice is on the side of the returning sinner. First John 1:9 says, "If we confess our sins, he is faithful and just to forgive us our sins, and to cleanse us from all unrighteousness." Justice is over on our side now because the mystery of the agony of God on the cross has changed our moral situation. So justice looks and sees equality, not inequity, and we are justified. That's what justification means.

Do I believe in justification by faith? Oh, my brother, do I believe in it! David believed in it and wrote it into Psalm 32. It was later quoted by one of the prophets. It was picked up by Paul and written into Galatians and Romans. It was lost for a while and relegated to the dust bin and then brought out again to the forefront and taught by Luther and the Moravians and the Wesleys and the Presbyterians. "Justification by faith"—we stand on it today.

When we talk about justification, it isn't just a text to manipulate. We ought to see who God is and see why these things are true. We're justified by faith because the agony of God on the cross changed the moral situation. We are that moral situation. It didn't change God at all. The idea that the cross wiped the angry scowl off the face of God and He began grudgingly to smile is a pagan concept and not Christian.

God is one. Not only is there only one God, but that one God is unitary, one with Himself, indivisible. And the mercy of God is simply God being merciful. And the justice of God is simply God being just. And the love of God is simply God loving. And the compassion of God is simply God being compassionate. It's not something that runs out of God—it's something God is!

THE UNCHANGING GOD

How can God be just and still justify a sinner? There is a third answer. Compassion flows from goodness, and yet goodness without justice is not goodness. You couldn't be good and not be just, and if God is good He has to be just. When God punishes the wicked, it is a just thing to do, because it is consistent with the wicked man's deserts. But when God pardons a wicked man it is a just thing to do as well, because it is consistent with God's nature. So we have God the Father, Son, and Holy Ghost always acting like God. Your wife may be grouchy, your best friend may be cold, foreign wars may be going on, but God is always the same. Always God acts according to His attributes of love, justice, and mercy.

Always, always, always God acts like God. Aren't you glad you aren't going to sneak into heaven through a cellar window? Aren't you glad that you're not going to get in like some preachers get academic degrees, by paying twenty-five dollars to a diploma factory?

Aren't you glad that you're not going to get into heaven by God's oversight? God is so busy with His world that you sneak in. You're there a thousand years before God sees you!

Aren't you glad that you're not going to get in just by being a member of a church? God says, "Well, that's a pretty good church. Let's let him in." And so you go in, but later on He finds your rotten spots and maybe you'll be thrown out!

There is the parable of the man who appeared without a wedding garment. And after he got in, they said, "What is he doing here?" and they threw him out—bound him hand and foot, lugged him out and threw him into outer darkness (see Matt. 22:11–13). There'll be nothing like that in God's kingdom, because God, the All-Wise One, knows all that can be known. He knows everybody—He knows you. And God, the All-Just One, will never permit the unequal man in there. "Why walk ye along on two unequal legs?" said Elijah (paraphrase of 1 Kings 18:21). That's unequal iniquity. And the man who is iniquitous will never get in. Never!

All of this cheap talk about St. Peter giving us an exam to see if we're all right—it's all nonsense! The Great God Almighty, always one with Himself, looks upon a moral situation and He either sees death or life. And all of God is on the side of death or life. If there is an iniquitous, unequal, unatoned, uncleansed, unprotected sinner in his sin, there's only one answer—all of God says, "Death and hell." And all of heaven can't pull that man up.

But if he beats his breast and says, "God be merciful to me a sinner" (Luke 18:13), and takes the benefits of the infinite agony of God on a cross, God looks on that moral situation and says, "Life!" And all of hell can't drag that man down. Oh, the wonder and the mystery and the glory of the being of God!

REFLECT

1. How does knowing that Christ's sacrificial death was infinite, almighty, and perfect shape the way you see your sin and God's forgiveness?

2. Why do you think so many people supposed Jesus' death on the cross changed God from being angry to loving? How does Tozer help us to see God rightly in this regard?

11

OUR MEDIATOR

Just as people are destined to die once, and after that to face judgment, so Christ was sacrificed once to take away the sins of many; and he will appear a second time, not to bear sin, but to bring salvation to those who are waiting for him.

HEBREWS 9:27–28

I am amazed by the number of people who do not seem to know that the Bible speaks of two forms of death. We believe the Bible when it says physical death is the reality facing every person born into the world. But there is also a very evident condition among us described as spiritual death. We trace it back to the Garden of Eden and the warning of God to our first parents: "Of every tree of the garden thou mayest freely eat: but of the tree of the knowledge of good and evil, thou shalt not eat of it: for in the day that thou eatest thereof thou shalt surely die" (Gen. 2:16–17). Adam and Eve did not heed the warning; they ate of the forbidden fruit. And on the day that they transgressed the law of God in disobedience and self-will, they died spiritually.

Death is not annihilation. Death is not cessation of existence. Death is a changed relationship in a different form of existence.

When Satan, a creation of God, rebelled in pride and disobedience, he was saying, "I will arise and put my throne above the throne of God!" And right there Satan died. But he did not cease to be. God expelled him from heaven and from fellowship with Himself. He cast him down to earth. And after all these centuries, Satan is still around. He was not annihilated, and his eternal judgment is still to come.

Men and women try to ignore the fact of spiritual death. The Scriptures do not. Paul has a classic one-sentence commentary on the subject. He says to the woman, "But she that liveth in pleasure is dead while she liveth" (1 Tim. 5:6). She was not dead physically, but spiritually she was cut off from God. Her form of existence was such that she was not related to, but separated from, God.

The apostle also warns us that death is one of sin's fearful consequences. Sin came into the world and brought death with it. The soul that sins will die. So the Bible declares.

SIN ENDS IN DEATH

Another thing we see in the Hebrews Scripture earlier quoted is that God has a very simple way of dealing with sin. God terminates sin in death! I lived in Chicago when the notorious killer gangster John Dillinger was being hunted. The police printed pictures of Dillinger with warnings about his violence with guns. Always he was shown with a cynical, sarcastic smile on his face. But the final picture indicated that he had stopped sinning. He was lying on his back, toes up. He was covered with a sheet. Dillinger was dead.

Sin ends at death. When a person dies, he or she will sin no more. That is God's way of ending sin. He lets death terminate it.

God's Word makes it clear that the life touched and tainted with sin is a forfeited life. The soul that sins shall die. The wonder that we will never fully understand is that God wanted to save our forfeited lives. So He allowed the blood of the divine Savior to be offered on our behalf. Notice that there must be a blood atonement because blood and life have a vital, mysterious relationship.

The blood of Jesus Christ is of infinite value. The pouring out of blood indicates the termination of life. Because the blood of Jesus Christ, the eternal Son, the Lamb of God, was poured out, our acts of sin may be pardoned.

We need to give this spiritual truth all the reverence and contemplation it deserves. Do we talk too loosely about the price of our redemption? I confess that I cringe just a little when I hear someone speak about Christ paying our debt—buying us back. Sometimes we make it sound like nothing more than a business deal. But I do not like to think of God redeeming us in the way we might redeem a cow or a horse at some livestock show. In God's plan for redeeming us there is something higher and holier, sweeter and more beautiful.

In the Old Testament, the sacrifices and offerings and the poured-out blood of animals were efficacious in ceremonial symbolism. But the death of Jesus Christ was efficacious actually and eternally. (*Efficacious* is a word theologians like to use; it simply means that it works. It is effective. You can count on it.) When Jesus poured out His blood on Calvary, He guaranteed eternal redemption to all who would put their trust in Him.

The blood and the life are one. When the blood was poured out, when Jesus Christ the eternal Son died, His death became vicarious. (*Vicarious* is another word that needs a brief explanation. A vicarious act is one performed on behalf of someone else. When Jesus died at Calvary, it was a vicarious death. Jesus died on behalf of us all, the innocent One for the guilty many.)

The atoning, vicarious death of Jesus Christ for sinful humanity is at the very foundation of the Christian faith. For those who think they can find a better way than God's way, it is not a popular teaching. But there is no other way. Jesus is the only way.

RECONCILED TO GOD

If you are a believing, trusting, joyful Christian, never let anyone rob you of this assurance and consolation. Allow no one to edit or change this basic truth—trying to make it more acceptable to philosophy or literature or art or religion. Let this wonderful truth stand tall in its beauty and effectiveness. Christ died, and in the giving of His life, He died vicariously!

In Christ's atoning death, the holiness and justice of God have been satisfied. God no longer holds anything against us, for we have come to Him in faith. We have pleaded as our merit only the vicarious, efficacious death of our Savior and Lord. And as we have believed, we have found the power of death broken.

The writer of the letter to the Hebrews assures us that Jesus has become the Mediator—the executor—of the new covenant, the new testament in God's grace and mercy. The word *mediator* comes from the verb "to mediate." A mediator is one who stands between two parties or two factions needing to be reconciled.

The Bible lets us know how far sinful mankind is from a holy God. Sin has dug a vast separating gulf. Christ has become the Mediator. By the giving of Himself in death, He stands between God and sinners. He shows us that by His death He has made effective God's testament, God's will.

That contract into which God has entered guarantees reconciliation. We are reconciled to God! God's gracious new will— His contract—guarantees pardon. We may be restored into the household of God by faith.

NAMED IN GOD'S WILL

Let me share with you another observation simple in concept but profound in this context of our divine inheritance. As long as the Lord Jesus lived, God's new covenant and will for us could not become effective. It became immediately effective the instant Christ died. The death of the Testator brought immediate pardon, forgiveness, cleansing, fellowship, and the promise of eternal life. Such is the bountiful and enduring legacy that has come by faith to the believing children of God as a result of Jesus' Calvary death.

I want to conclude by pointing out something that will sound strange to any mortal human being. No man ever died to make his will valid and then came back to earth as the executor of his will. No one. Some other person always acts as executor and administrator of the estate that has been left.

But what no mortal has done, Jesus Christ, the eternal Son of God, has achieved. He has accomplished this kind of enduring administration and divine beneficence. Jesus died to activate the terms of the will to all its beneficiaries; Jesus rose in victory from the grave to administer the will.

Is that not beautiful? Jesus did not turn God's will over to someone else to administer. He Himself became the Administrator. Many times He declared, "I will be back. I will rise again on the third day!" He came back from the dead. He rose on the third day. He lives to carry out for His people all the terms of His will.

We must continue to trust this Living One who is now our great High Priest in the heavens. There is not a single argument in liberal theology strong enough to pry us from our faith. We have a living hope in this world, and that living hope is equally valid for the world to come.

Oh, yes. I should tell you exactly who are named in God's new will.

The answer is Christ's answer and invitation. Whosoever! "Whoever wishes, let him take the free gift." Amen.

REFLECT

1. Why does God no longer hold our sins against us if we trust in Him?

2. What do you think of Tozer's explanation for the assurance we have in Christ's redeeming sacrifice?

3. How exactly do we benefit from Christ's death?

12

THE RESURRECTION

*The angel said to the women, "Do not be afraid, for
I know that you are looking for Jesus, who was crucified.
He is not here; he has risen, just as he said. Come
and see the place where he lay. Then go quickly and
tell his disciples: 'He has risen from the dead and is going
ahead of you into Galilee. There you will see him.'"*

MATTHEW 28:5–7

Any Christian church that looks back to the crucifixion only with sorry tears and that is not pressing forward in the blessed life of the risen Christ, is no more than a "pitying kind of religion."

And I must agree with one of the old writers in the faith who said, "I cannot away with it!"—meaning, "I cannot tolerate this pitying kind of religion."

True spiritual power does not reside in the ancient cross but rather in the victory of the mighty, resurrected Lord of glory, who could pronounce after spoiling death: "All power is given unto me in heaven and in earth!" (Matt. 28:18)

Let us be confident, Christian brethren, that our power does not lie in the manger at Bethlehem nor in the relics of the cross.

The power of the believer lies in the triumph of eternal glory!

The Man who died on the cross died in weakness. The Bible is plain in telling us this. But He arose in power. If we forget or deny the truth and glory of His resurrection and the fact that He is seated at the right hand of God, we lose all the significance of the meaning of Christianity!

A CHANGE OF DIRECTION

The resurrection of Jesus Christ brought about a startling change of direction. It is interesting and profitable to look at the direction of the prepositions in Matthew's account of the resurrection morning.

First, the women came to the tomb.

They came in love, but they came in sadness and fear, and they came to mourn. That was the direction of their religion before they knew Jesus had been raised from the dead. Their direction was toward the grave—the tomb that held the body of Jesus.

Many who still face in the direction of the tomb, knowing only mourning and grief, uncertainty and the fear of death, are all around us.

But on that historic resurrection day, the faithful women had a dramatic change of direction.

They heard the angelic news and they saw the evidence: "He is not here: for he is risen, as he said!" (Matt. 28:6). The mammoth stone had been rolled away and they themselves could see the stark emptiness of the tomb.

"Go quickly, and tell His disciples!"

So the record tells us they departed immediately from the sepulcher.

What an amazing change of direction! What a change wrought by the joyful news!

The preposition is now *from* the grave instead of *to* the grave. The direction is suddenly away from the tomb—because the tomb was empty and stripped of its age-old power.

The direction is suddenly no longer toward the end—for with Jesus alive from the dead and about to be glorified at the right hand of the Father, the direction changed toward endlessness— the eternity of eternal life and victory!

If this is not the message and meaning of Easter, the Christian church is involved in a shallow one-day festival each year, intent upon the brightness of colors and the fragrance of flowers and the sweet sentiments of poetry and springtime.

The Christian church should have its priorities in the right order.

Easter is not just a day in the church calendar, something to be celebrated each year as an end in itself, something that began early on that first day of the week and ended at midnight.

The resurrection morning was only the beginning of a great, grand, and vast outreach that has never ended and will not end until our Lord Jesus Christ comes back again.

The reality of Easter and of the resurrection and of the great commission of the risen and ascending Christ is the reality of the great missionary priority of the Christian church throughout today's world.

The resurrection of Christ and the fact of the empty tomb are not a part of the world's complex and continuing mythologies. This is not a Santa Claus tale—it is history and it is reality.

The Christian church is helpless and hopeless if it is stripped of the reality and historicity of the bodily resurrection of Jesus Christ. The true church of Jesus Christ is necessarily founded upon the belief and the truth that it happened. There was a real death, there was a real tomb, there was a real stone. But, thank God, there was a sovereign Father in heaven, an angel sent to roll the stone away, and a living Savior in a resurrected and glorified body able to proclaim to His disciples, "All power is given unto me in heaven and in earth!"

Since that is our prospect and hope, there is no reason for any of us to be continually asking for pity for the Lord Jesus Christ.

The church has too many radiant, beckoning opportunities to be occupied with this: "Let us kneel down by the cross and let us weep awhile."

It is wrong for us to join those whose concept seems to be that our Lord was a martyr, a victim of His own zeal, a poor pitiable Man with good intentions who found the world too big and life too much for Him. He is still portrayed by too many as sinking down in a helplessness wrought by death.

Why should we in His church walk around in black and continue to grieve at the tomb when the record clearly shows that He came back from death to prove His words: "All power is given unto me in heaven and in earth!"

WHERE THE POWER IS

Brethren, He died for us, but ever since the hour of resurrection, He has been the mighty Jesus, the mighty Christ, the mighty Lord!

Power does not lie with a babe in the manger.

Power does not lie with a man nailed and helpless on a cross.

Power lies with the man on that cross who gave His life, who went into the grave and who arose and came out on the third day, then to ascend to the right hand of the Father.

That is where power lies.

Our business is not to mourn and weep beside the grave.

Our business is to thank God with tearful reverence that He once was willing to go into that grave. Our business is to thank God for the understanding of what the cross meant and for understanding of what the resurrection meant both to God and to men.

Do we rightly understand the resurrection, in the sense that it placed a glorious crown upon all of Christ's sufferings?

Do we realize the full significance of our Lord Jesus Christ being seated today at the Father's right hand, seated in absolute majesty and kingly power, sovereign over every power in heaven and in earth?

There is always someone with a rejoinder: "But, Mr. Tozer, how can you back up that big talk? If Christ is sovereign over all the world, what about the world condition?

"What about Russia and spreading Communism?

"What about atom bombs and hydrogen bombs and impending doom?

"If He is sovereign, why is there a continuing armament race? Why does the Middle East situation continue to plague the entire world?"

There is an answer and it is the answer of the prophetic Scripture.

God has a prophetic plan in His dealing with the world, its nations, and its governments.

God's plan will continue on God's schedule. His plan has always called for the return of Israel to Palestine. The nations of the earth are playing themselves into position all over the world—almost like a giant checkerboard—while God waits for the consummation.

While Israel gathers and while the King of the North beats himself out, the Christian church prays and labors to evangelize the world for the Savior.

Christ waits—even though He has all the power. He waits to exercise His awesome power.

He is showing His power in many ways in the life and ministries of His church.

I believe He would exercise His unlimited power if His church would truly believe that He could and would do it!

When Jesus announced that "all power is given unto me in heaven and in earth," what did He expect His followers to do? What are the implications for all of us who are in the body of Christ?

The answer is plain; Jesus said, "Go ye, therefore!"

Therefore is the word that connects everything together. Christ has been given all power; therefore we are to go and evangelize, discipling all nations. All of the implications of the resurrection add up to the fact that the Christian church must be a missionary church if it is to meet the expectations of the risen Savior!

Because He is alive forevermore, Jesus could promise, in the same context as His command, that He would be with us always, even unto the end of the world, or age.

There have been many little wall plaques and mottoes on display in Christian homes reading: "Lo, I am with you always, even unto the end of the world." But that is only a partial quotation and it overrides certain implications.

You know how skillfully we take the knife of bad teaching and separate a little passage from the context even as we might take the rind from an orange. We peel the promise off and put it on our mottoes and calendars.

Let's be truthful and let our Lord say to us all exactly what He wants to say.

Is this what He said, "Lo, I am with you always"?

Not exactly, my brother.

He actually said, "Go ye therefore, and teach all nations, baptizing them in the name of the Father, and of the Son, and of the Holy Ghost: Teaching them to observe all things whatsoever I have commanded you: and, lo, I am with you always, even unto the end of the world" (Matt. 28:19–20).

That little word *and* is not there by accident. Jesus literally was saying that His presence was promised and assured in the Christian church if the church continued faithful in its missionary responsibilities.

That's why I say that the resurrection of Jesus Christ is something more than making us the happiest fellows in the Easter parade.

Am I to listen to a cantata and join in singing "Up from the grave He arose," smell the flowers, and go home and forget it?

No, certainly not!

DEMONSTRATING THE RESURRECTION

It is truth and a promise with a specific moral application. The resurrection certainty lays hold on us with all the authority of sovereign obligation.

It says that the Christian church is to go—to go into all the world, reaching and teaching all nations, or as the margin has it, "Make disciples among all nations."

So, the moral obligation of the resurrection of Christ is the missionary obligation, the responsibility and the privilege of carrying the message and telling the story, of praying and interceding, and of being involved personally and financially in the cause of this great commission.

I have asked myself many times why professing Christian believers can relegate the great missionary imperative of our Lord Jesus Christ to the sidelines of our Christian cause.

I cannot follow the reasoning of those who teach that the missionary commission given by Jesus Christ does not belong to the church but will be carried out during the great tribulation days emphasized in Bible prophecy.

I cannot give in to the devil's principal, deceitful tactic that makes so many Christians satisfied with an Easter celebration instead of experiencing the power of His resurrection. The enemy of our souls is quite happy about the situation when Christians make a big deal of Easter Sunday, put the emphasis on flowers and cantatas, and preachers use their soft-voiced and dewy-eyed technique in referring to Jesus as the greatest of all earth's heroes.

The devil is willing to settle for all of that kind of display as long as the churches stop short of telling the whole truth about the resurrection of Christ.

"It's fine with me if they just make a big hero of Jesus, but I don't ever want them to remember for a minute that He is now seated in the place of power and I am actually a poor, frightened fugitive"—that's the reasoning of the devil.

And it is his business to keep Christians mourning awhile and weeping with pity beside the tree instead of demonstrating that Jesus Christ is risen indeed, is at the right hand of the Father in glory, and has the right and authority to put the devil in hell when the time comes, chaining him and hurling him down according to God's revealed prophetic plan.

The devil will do almost anything to keep us from actually believing and trusting that death has no more dominion and that Jesus Christ has been given all authority in heaven and in earth and hell, holding the keys thereof.

When will the Christian church rise up and get on the offensive for the risen and ascended Savior?

When we come to know the full meaning of the cross and experience the meaning and the power of the resurrection in our own lives—that is the answer. Through the power of His resurrection we will take the spiritual offensive; we become the aggressors and our witness and testimony become the positive force in reaching the ends of the earth with the gospel.

We can just sum it all up by noting that Jesus Christ asks us only to surrender to His Lordship and obey His commands. He will supply the power if we will believe His promise and demonstrate the reality of His resurrection.

These promises of Christ have taken all the strain and pressure from our missionary responsibility. When the Spirit of God speaks and deals with our young people about their own missionary responsibility, Christ assures them of His presence and power as they prepare to go.

"All power is given unto Me. I am no longer in the grave. With all authority and power I can protect you, I can support you, I can go ahead of you, I can give you effectiveness in your witness and ministry. Go, therefore, and make disciples of all nations, and I will go with you. I will never leave you nor forsake you!"

Men without God suffer alone and die alone in time of war and in other circumstances of life. All alone!

But it can never be said that any true soldier of the cross of Jesus Christ, no man or woman as missionary or messenger of the truth has ever gone out to a ministry alone!

There have been many Christian martyrs—but not one of them was on that mission field all alone. No missionary that ever laid down his life in the jungle was actually alone—for Jesus Christ keeps His promise of taking him by the hand and leading him triumphantly through to the world beyond.

Do you see it, my friend? Resurrection is not a day of celebration—it is an obligation understood and accepted!

Because Jesus Christ is alive, there is something for us to do for Him every day. We cannot just sit down, settling back in religious apathy.

We can dare to fully trust the Risen One who said, "All power is given unto me in heaven and in earth . . . go ye therefore . . . and, lo, I am with you always, even unto the end of the world."

REFLECT

1. What would your life look like if you lived in greater awareness of the power of Christ's resurrection?

2. Have you ever considered that Christian mission is connected to the resurrection? How does this knowledge impact the way you live your life day to day?

3. What would demonstrating the reality of the resurrection look like in your own life?

THE ASCENDED LORD

He was taken up before their very eyes,
and a cloud hid him from their sight.

Acts 1:9

O ur forgiveness and cleansing by the once-and-for-all sacrifice of Jesus Christ is only part of the good news. Jesus died, but He rose from the dead. And after His resurrection, He ascended to be seated at the right hand of the Majesty in heaven. In an era of declining morality and open rebellion against God and against His Anointed One, we can take great comfort in this revelation that a majestic, overruling Presence resides in glory.

The Majesty still fills the throne room of heaven. The angels and archangels and seraphim and cherubim continue their celestial praise of "Holy, holy, holy, Lord God Almighty." This is not some far-out concept of some fringe cult. This is straight from the Word of God: When Jesus "had by himself purged our sins, sat down on the right hand of the Majesty on high" (Heb. 1:3).

Jesus returned to the position He had occupied throughout the long, long ages past.

A REAL MAN IN HEAVEN

An earnest Christian worker and serious student of the Bible with whom I have had correspondence laments the fact that our Christian preaching and teaching does not more clearly identify the risen, ascended Jesus as a Man. He has questioned preachers and Christian teachers, many of them well known, "Do you believe that Jesus Christ, now at God's right hand, is a man, or some other being?" Very few of these Christian leaders purportedly believe that Jesus is now a glorified Man. They believe Jesus was a man while He was here on earth, but they tend to believe that He is a spirit now.

After Jesus' resurrection from the dead, He appeared to His disciples. He invited Thomas to feel the wound marks in His flesh. What blessed meaning there is in His words to the fearful disciples: "Behold my hands and my feet, that it is I myself: handle me, and see; for a spirit hath not flesh and bones, as ye see me have" (Luke 24:39).

Whether modern men and women agree on the exaltation of the Man Christ Jesus, we in the family of God have heard His words and we know the New Testament witness: "This Jesus hath God raised up, whereof we all are witnesses. Therefore being by the right hand of God exalted, and having received of the Father the promise of the Holy Ghost, he hath shed forth this, which ye now see and hear" (Acts 2:32–33).

The apostle Paul told Timothy, "For there is one God, and

one mediator between God and men, the man Christ Jesus; who gave himself a ransom for all, to be testified in due time" (1 Tim. 2:5–6). This should be counted as a great victory for Christian believers in our day. Jesus is a Man and He is enthroned at God's right hand. That is significant!

JOINED TO JESUS

Jesus is not said to be the victorious God—God is always victorious. How could the sovereign God be anything but victorious? Rather, we take our position with those earliest Christian believers who saw in Jesus a Man in the heavenlies. He is a victorious Man, and if we are in Him, we too can be victorious.

Through the new birth, the miracle of regeneration, we have been brought by faith into the kingdom of God. As Christians we should recognize that our nature has been joined to God's nature in the mystery of the incarnation. Jesus has done everything He can to make His unbelieving people see that we have the same place in the heart of God that He Himself has. He does so not because we are worthy of it, but because He is worthy and He is the Head of the Church. He is the representative Man before God, representing us.

Jesus is the model Man after which we are patterned in our Christian faith and fellowship. That is why He will not let us alone. He is determined that we will have eyes to see more than this world around us. He is determined that we will have eyes of faith to see God in the kingdom of heaven, and Himself—our Man in glory—seated there in victorious control!

BELIEVE EVERY TRUTH

At the risk of sounding more than slightly repetitious, I want to urge again that we Christians look to our doctrinal emphases.

If we would know the power of truth we must emphasize it. Creedal truth is coal lying inert in the depths of the earth waiting release. Dig it out, shovel it into the combustion chamber of some huge engine, and the mighty energy that lay asleep for centuries will create light and heat and cause the machinery of a great factory to surge into productive action. The theory of coal never turned a wheel nor warmed a hearth. Power must be released to be made effective.

In the redemptive work of Christ three major epochs may be noted: His birth, His death, and His subsequent elevation to the right hand of God. These are the three main pillars that uphold the temple of Christianity; upon them rest all the hopes of mankind, world without end. All else that He did takes its meaning from these three Godlike deeds.

It is imperative that we believe all these truths, but the big question is where to lay the emphasis. Which truth should, at a given time, receive the sharpest accent? We are exhorted to look unto Jesus, but where shall we look? Unto Jesus in the manger? on the cross? at the throne? These questions are far from academic. It is of great practical importance to us that we get the right answer.

Of course we must include in our total creed the manger, the cross, and the throne. All that is symbolized by these three objects must be present to the gaze of faith; all is necessary to a proper understanding of the Christian evangel. No single tenet of our creed must be abandoned or even relaxed, for each is joined to the other by a living bond. But while all truth is at all times to be held inviolate, not every truth is to be at all times emphasized equally with every other. Our Lord indicated as much when He spoke of the faithful and wise steward who gave to his master's household "their portion of meat in due season" (Luke 12:42).

Mary brought forth her firstborn Son and wrapped Him in swaddling clothes and laid Him in a manger. Wise men came to worship, shepherds wondered, and angels chanted of peace and good will toward men. All taken together this scene is so chastely beautiful, so winsome, so tender, that the like of it is not found anywhere in the literature of the world. It is not hard to see why Christians have tended to place such emphasis upon the manger, the meek-eyed virgin, and the Christ-child. In certain Christian circles the major emphasis is made to fall upon the child in the manger. Why this is so is understandable, but the emphasis is nevertheless misplaced.

Christ was born that He might become a man and became a man that He might give His life as ransom for many. Neither the birth nor the dying were ends in themselves. As He was born to die, so did He die that He might atone, and rise that He might justify freely all who take refuge in Him. His birth and His death are history. His appearance at the mercy seat is not history past, but a present, continuing fact, to the instructed Christian the most glorious fact his trusting heart can entertain. . . .

LOOKING TO WHERE CHRIST IS

Let us remember that weakness lies at the manger, death at the cross, and power at the throne. Our Christ is not in a manger.

Indeed, New Testament theology nowhere presents the Christ-child as an object of saving faith. The gospel that stops at the manger is another gospel and no good news at all.

The Church that still gathers around the manger can only be weak and misty-eyed, mistaking sentimentality for the power of the Holy Spirit.

As there is now no babe in the manger at Bethlehem so there is no man on the cross at Jerusalem. To worship the babe in the manger or the man on the cross is to reverse the redemptive processes of God and turn the clock back on His eternal purposes. Let the Church place its major emphasis upon the cross and there can be only pessimism, gloom, and fruitless remorse. Let a sick man die hugging a crucifix and what have we there? Two dead men in a bed, neither of which can help the other.

The glory of the Christian faith is that the Christ who died for our sins rose again for our justification. We should joyfully remember His birth and gratefully muse on His dying, but the crown of all our hopes is with Him at the Father's right hand.

Paul gloried in the cross and refused to preach anything except Christ and Him crucified, but to him the cross stood for the whole redemptive work of Christ. In his epistles, Paul writes of the incarnation and the crucifixion, yet he stops not at the manger or the cross but constantly sweeps our thoughts on to the resurrection and upward to the ascension and the throne.

"All power is given unto me in heaven and in earth" (Matt. 28:18), said our risen Lord before He went up on high, and the first Christians believed Him and went forth to share His triumph. "With great power gave the apostles witness of the resurrection of the Lord Jesus: and great grace was upon them all" (Acts 4:33).

Should the Church shift her emphasis from the weakness of the manger and the death of the cross to the life and power of the enthroned Christ, perhaps she might recapture her lost glory. It is worth a try.

REFLECT

1. Why is it significant that Jesus as a real human being is present in heaven?

2. How does Tozer's description of Jesus in this chapter alter your perception of who He is and what He does?

3. If all our hopes are built upon three main pillars, what kind of hope does the epoch of Christ's ascension into heaven give us?

4. Does your own thinking about Christ and His ministry need to take a shift?

14

OUR HIGH PRIEST

*Therefore, since we have a great high priest who
has ascended into heaven, Jesus the Son of God,
let us hold firmly to the faith we profess.*

HEBREWS 4:14

It was never in the mind of God that a privileged priesthood of sinful, imperfect men would attempt, following the death and triumphant resurrection of our Lord Jesus Christ, to repair the veil and continue their office of mediation between God and man. The letter to the Hebrews makes that fact very plain. When Jesus rose from the dead, the Levitical priesthood, which had served Israel under the old covenant, became redundant.

God's better plan for an eternal High Priest and a sinless Mediator is also made plain in the letter to the Hebrews. Jesus glorified at the right hand of the Majesty in the heavens is now our High Priest forever. His priesthood is not after the order of Aaron and Levi but after the enduring priesthood of Melchizedek.

Those are highlights in the Hebrews message concerning the better covenant, the better priesthood, and the better hope resting upon the completed work of Jesus Christ for lost mankind. We read:

> Jesus, made an high priest for ever after the order of Melchisedec. . . . For the priesthood being changed, there is made of necessity a change also of the law. . . . For there is verily a disannulling of the commandment going before for the weakness and unprofitableness thereof. For the law made nothing perfect, but the bringing in of a better hope did; by the which we draw nigh unto God. . . . For if that first covenant had been faultless, then should no place have been sought for the second. (Heb. 6:20; 7:12, 18–19; 8:7)

Long before the time of Moses and Aaron and the sons of Levi, the Genesis record notes the appearance of a mysterious yet compelling personality, Melchizedek. Melchizedek was king of Salem and priest of the most high God. When Abraham returned from the rescue of Lot, his nephew, he was greeted and blessed by Melchizedek. And Abraham gave to Mechizedek the tithe of all the goods he had recovered (Genesis 14:17–20).

The Genesis appearance of Melchizedek is brief and without explanation in Old Testament history. More information is offered by the writer to the Hebrews. When he notes that Melchizedek was "without father, without mother, without descent, having neither beginning of days, nor end of life" (Heb. 7:3), the writer simply was saying that Melchizedek had no "family tree," no genealogical records through which his origins could be traced. In short, we do not know where he came from.

Melchizedek is not mentioned again until Psalm 110. There he is referred to as the type of an eternal priest of God who would yet appear in Israel's national development.

Jews were very meticulous about genealogy. Each son or daughter of Israel could trace his or her ancestry back to Abraham. It is only too apparent that later generations in Israel did not know how to deal with the references to Melchizedek, a priest whose lineage they could not trace.

The reason all Jews so jealously guarded their lineage, preserving these on permanent tablets, was related to their hope of Messiah's coming. They knew the prophecies. When Messiah finally appeared, He would have to prove His line of descent from Abraham through King David and on down to His own parents.

In his New Testament Gospel, Matthew conformed to Jewish custom, taking pains to furnish his readers a full record of the genealogy of Jesus Christ. He begins with Abraham, Isaac, and Jacob, carries the lineage through David and Solomon to another Jacob, concluding with "Joseph the husband of Mary, of whom was born Jesus, who is called Christ" (Matt. 1:16).

In view of the importance given to the Jewish records of ancestry, it is significant that all those carefully preserved records were lost in the Roman destruction of Jerusalem in AD 70—so historians believe. Jesus had come as Redeemer and Messiah. Israel rejected Him, crucifying Him on the cross. But there could be no other. No other could have furnished the necessary proof of his descent from Abraham and David. Jesus, the risen, ascended Son of God was and is Israel's final hope.

AN INFINITELY
BETTER PRIESTHOOD

As we come into a consideration of the things taught in this section of Hebrews, we must be prepared to do some thinking. We live in a generation that wants everything condensed and predigested. But here we must do some thinking. And in the end, the understanding we achieve will be well worth the effort.

In this part of his letter, the writer sets out to make three things very plain to the troubled Hebrew Christians of his day. First, he declares that the Mosaic law and the Levitical priesthood were not established by God as permanent and perfect institutions. Second, he makes it plain that the eternal and sinless Son came to assure believers concerning His superior and enduring priesthood, confirmed by His glorification at God's right hand. Third, he wants his readers to know that the plan of salvation for sinful men and women does not rest upon earthly offerings made by Levitical priests, but upon the eternal sacrifice and high priestly mediation of Jesus, the eternal Son, who also was willing to become the sacrificial Lamb of God.

The comparisons made in this letter indicate that the provisions of the Old Testament Mosaic law and the system of the Levitical priesthood were interdependent. Thus, when the priesthood was eliminated, the Mosaic law passed away also. The writer's summary is clear: "For there is verily a disannulling of the commandment going before for the weakness and unprofitableness thereof. For the law made nothing perfect, but the bringing in of a better hope did; by the which we draw nigh unto God" (Heb. 7:18–19).

FREE IN CHRIST

What does all this mean to us in our Christian lives, our Christian faith? Thankfully, it means that we do not stand under the shadow of those laws given through Moses. We do not stand under the shadow of the imperfections of the Old Testament Jewish priesthood and mediation. Instead, we stand in the light and authority of Jesus Christ. He is superior to all Old Testament priests. He has fulfilled the law—dismissed it, if you will—by the institution of the new covenant based on a superior sacrifice.

This new covenant, sealed in the blood of Jesus, our Savior and Mediator, introduces for us a great spiritual freedom. We should rejoice daily. No one can lay the burden of the old law upon us—a law that Israel was unable to fulfill.

In his letter to the church in Galatia, Paul dealt with this very problem. He states the principle of God's grace and righteousness through faith with telling effect. He condemns those who followed the Galatian Christians around, trying to make Jews out of them. "Stand fast therefore," he says, "in the liberty wherewith Christ hath made us free, and be not entangled again with the yoke of bondage. . . . Christ is become of no effect unto you, whosoever of you are justified by the law; ye are fallen from grace" (Gal. 5:1, 4).

We who are Christian believers should thank God continually for our New Testament guarantees of spiritual life and freedom in Christ! Our sacrifice is not an animal offered by a priest as imperfect as we are. Our sacrifice is the very Lamb of God, who was able and willing to offer Himself to take away the sins of the world. Our altar is not the altar in old Jerusalem.

Our altar is Calvary, where Jesus offered Himself without spot to God through the eternal Spirit. Our Holy of Holies is not that section of a temple made with hands, secluded behind a protective veil. Our Holy of Holies is in heaven, where the exalted Jesus sits at the right hand of the Majesty on high.

A NEW SACRIFICE

Note the comparison of the two priesthoods. In the Old Testament, every priest who ever served knew that he would ultimately be retired and die. Each priest was temporal. But in our Lord Jesus Christ we have an eternal High Priest. He has explored and conquered death. He will not die again. He will continue as a priest forever, and He will never change! It is for that very reason, the writer assures us, that Jesus is "able also to save them to the uttermost that come unto God by him, seeing he ever liveth to make intercession for them" (Heb. 7:25).

Before we move on from the subject of the passing of the Old Testament priestly mediation, I want to mention the strange, anomalous event that took place within the Jerusalem temple as Jesus gave up His life on the cross. As He "gave up the ghost" (John 19:30) outside Jerusalem, the very finger of God Almighty reached into the temple's most holy place, splitting, rending, tearing the heavy hanging veil (Matt. 27:51).

That ancient veil was not just a curtain. It was a special drape—a veil so thick and heavy that it took several men to pull it aside. As Jesus died, the finger of God rent that veil that had housed the earthly presence of the invisible God. Thus, God was indicating the beginning of a new covenant and a new relationship between mankind and Himself. He was demonstrating the passing of the old order and the transfer of authority, efficacy, and mediation to the new order.

The priesthood, the priests, the old covenants, the altars, the sacrifices—all that had been involved in the Old Testament system of law—was done away with. God had eliminated it as useless, powerless, without authority. In its place He instituted a new Sacrifice, the Lamb of God, the eternal Son, Jesus Christ. God instituted as well a new and efficacious altar, this one eternal in the heavens, where Jesus lives to intercede for God's believing children.

When the temple veil was torn top to bottom, tradition has it that the Levitical priests determined they must repair that long-sacred partition. And they did. They sewed it together as best they could. Not understanding that God had decreed a new order, they took the earthly view by trying to continue the old system of sacrifices.

I hope I will not be accused of anti-Semitism when I cite certain Bible truths indicating that even yet Jews do not really know why they worship. We evangelicals have no sympathy for those who hate the Jews. In our understanding of the Scriptures and God's great plan, we recognize the worth of our Jewish friends. We have a concern for their well-being in an unfriendly world.

Moreover, we believe strongly in the future glory of Israel. We believe that when God's Messiah returns, Israel will minister again in faith and worship in her own land. We believe in a day yet coming when a reborn Israel will shine forth. The Word of God's righteousness will go forth from Zion and the Word of God from Jerusalem.

But for the present, the living, beating life of Jewish faith is gone. There is no altar. There is no Shekinah glory and Presence. There is no efficacious sacrifice for sin. There is no mediatorial priest and no Holy of Holies for him to enter on behalf of his people. All is gone—eliminated as useless, powerless, without further authority.

In its place God has instituted and accepted a new sacrifice—the Lamb of God, the eternal Son. He has confirmed a new and efficacious altar, this one eternal in the heavens, where Jesus ever lives to make intercession for God's believing children. He has ordained and accepted a new High Priest, Jesus, the eternal Son, seating Him at His right hand.

All that I have been saying may seem complex and involved. This much we must understand: Jesus our Lord, God's Christ and our Savior, lives forevermore! As God is timeless and ageless, so also is Jesus Christ.

And Jesus lives to intercede for us! His eternal interest is to be our surety. We sing of it with faith and joy: "Before the throne my Surety stands; my name is written in His hands." And then we continue with the rest of those stirring words from the vision and heart of Charles Wesley:

> The Father hears Him pray,
> His dear anointed One;
> He cannot turn away
> The presence of His Son.
> His Spirit answers to the blood
> And tells me I am born of God.

It is Christ's unfailing intercession that makes it possible for us to tell each other that we believe in the security of the saints of God. We believe there is a place of security, not because there was some technicality that John Calvin might have advanced, but because of the high priestly intercession of the eternal One who cannot die. Day and night He offers our names before the Father in heaven. No matter how weak we may be, we are kept because Jesus Christ is our eternal High Priest in the heavens.

WHERE WE ARE GOING

How different is our vision of Jesus Christ from that of the ones who put Him to death, saying, "That is the end of him!" Our vision is of a risen, victorious, all-powerful, and all-wise High Priest. Quietly, triumphantly, He pleads the worth and value of His own life and blood for the preservation and victory of God's believing children.

Just consider, if you will, the gracious implications of God's guarantee. He declares in His Word that Jesus, our Savior and Mediator, "is able also to save them to the uttermost that come unto God by him, seeing he ever liveth to make intercession for them" (Heb. 7:25). There have been preachers who changed the preposition *to* and made it *from*. They preached a salvation with emphasis on what the individual sinner is saved from.

I heartily disagree with that emphasis!

Our Lord has given an invitation that excludes no one. "Whoever" is as broad as the human race. I do not believe God is concerned at all about where we have come from. He is concerned with where we are going. The decision we have made to go where we are going—to be with God forever—is what pleases Him and causes the angels to rejoice.

Some Christian workers have made an entire career of dwelling on the negative aspects of the human, sinful life—"from the uttermost." "Let me tell you what a hopeless drunkard I was!" "Attend the services and let me share what it is like to be a helpless drug addict!" "Come and let me relate the awful, tragic time in my past when I was a good-for-nothing wife-beater!"

It is a gracious thing that God does for us in His mercy and love when we are forgiven, regenerated, and converted. It is indeed a new birth! God saves us from what we were, whatever it was. But He expects us to spend the rest of our lives praising Him, telling about the wonders of Christ and His salvation. He wants us to spread the good news of the great eternal future He has planned for us. He wants us to tell others of the eternal habitation He is preparing for all who love and obey Him.

REFLECT

1. Are there any ways in which you have lost sight of the freedom you have in Christ?

2. Do you live your life knowing that you have instant access to God through the priestly ministry of Jesus?

3. How different would your life look if you contemplated more regularly the assurance you have of being with Christ in heaven someday?

EVER WITH US

For whenever you eat this bread and drink this cup,
you proclaim the Lord's death until he comes.

1 CORINTHIANS 11:26

It is amazing that many people seem to believe that the Christian church is just another institution and that the observance of communion is just one of its periodic rituals.

The Bible makes it plain that any church that is a genuine New Testament church is actually a communion and not an institution.

The dictionary says that a communion is a body of Christians having a common faith. Sharing and participation are other terms used in the definition of communion.

Regardless of traditions and terms and definition, the basic question in our coming to the Lord's table is this: "Have we come together to recognize the Presence of our divine Lord and risen Savior?"

Brethren, how wonderful if we have found the spiritual

maturity and understanding that allows us to confess: "Our congregation is so keenly aware of the presence of Jesus in our midst that our entire fellowship is an unceasing communion!"

What a joyful experience for us in this church age—to be part of a congregation drawn together with the magnetic fascination of the desire to know the presence of God and to sense His nearness.

The communion will not have ultimate meaning for us if we do not believe that our Lord Jesus Christ is literally present in the body of Christ on earth.

There is a distinction here: Christ is literally present with us—but not physically present.

Some people approach the communion table with an awe that is almost fear because they think they are approaching the physical presence of God. It is a mistake to imagine that He is physically present.

Remember that God was not physically present in the burning bush of the Old Testament. Neither was He physically present between the wings of the cherubim in the tabernacle, nor in the cloud by day and fire by night.

In all these instances, He was literally present.

And so today, God who became Man—the Man who is God—this Man who is the focal point of divine manifestation, is here!

When we come to the Lord's table, we do not have to try to bring His presence. He is here!

He does ask, however, that we bring the kind of faith that will know and discern His presence; the kind of faith that will enable us to forgive "one another, even as God for Christ's sake hath forgiven" us (Eph. 4:32).

Out of our worship and from the communion, God wants us to be able to sense the loving nearness of the Savior—instantaneously bestowed!

There is nothing else like this in the world—the Spirit of God standing ready with a baptism of the sense of the presence of the God who made heaven and earth and holds the world in His hands. Knowing the sense of His presence will completely change our everyday life. It will elevate us, purify us, and deliver us from the domination of carnal flesh to the point where our lives will be a continuing, radiant fascination!

Here I want to refer back to Paul's message to the Corinthian church. We read and understand that there was trouble in that early church because the members came together for reasons other than recognizing the divine Presence.

Paul said they met without "discerning the Lord's body."

I have checked many sources of Christian scholarship, and I agree with Ellicott and other commentaries who believe this means that they met "without recognizing the Presence."

They were not required to believe that the bread and wine *were* God, but they were required to believe that God was present *where* Christians met to serve the bread and wine. Because they refused to recognize His presence, they were in great spiritual trouble.

Actually, they were meeting together for purposes other than that of finding God at the focal point of manifestation in the person of His Son!

There was a judgment upon them because they were too carnal, too worldly, too socially minded, too unspiritual to recognize that when Christians meet they should at least have the reverence that a Greek had when he led a heifer to the sacred grove. They should at least have the reverence that a Greek poet had when he quietly composed sonnets to his deity. When they came together they ought to have at least the reverence of a Jewish high priest of the Old Testament when he approached the sacred holy place and put blood upon the mercy seat.

But they came with another attitude. They did not come to commune in the Presence, and so the purpose and meaning of communion became vague.

It was true in other churches as well as set forth in Revelation 2 and 3.

COMMEMORATING CHRIST

Today, I say, we ought to be a company of believers drawn together to see and hear and feel God appearing in man. That man is not a preacher, or elder, or deacon, but the Son of Man, Jesus Christ—back from the dead and eternally alive!

It is impossible to separate the communion table from the centrality of Jesus Christ in the revealed Word of God.

Some think of communion as a celebration—and in the very best sense it is our Lord Jesus Christ whom we celebrate when we come to this table.

In order for us to grasp the spirit of this commemoration, notice the relationship of Christ, the Son of Man, in five words with their prepositions attached.

First, we celebrate Christ's "devotion to"—noting, for instance, His devotion to the Father's will.

Our Lord Jesus Christ had no secondary aims. His one

passion in life was the fulfillment of His Father's will. Probably He was the only human being after the fall about whom this could be said in perfect terms. With any other person, it can be only an approximation. Realism requires that we say we suppose there never has been anyone who has not mourned the introduction, however brief, of some distraction.

But Jesus never had any distraction or deviation. His Father's will was always before Him, and it was to this one thing that He was devoted.

As part of that, He was devoted to the rescue of fallen mankind—completely devoted to it. He did not do a dozen other things as avocations. He did that one thing! He was devoted to the altar of sacrifice—to the rescue of mankind.

It may be helpful if I remind you about a famous symbol of one of the old Baptist missionary societies. It showed an ox quietly standing between an altar and a plow. Underneath was the legend, "Ready for either or for both!" Plow awhile, and then die on the altar. Or, only die on the altar or only plow awhile.

The meaning of the symbol was readiness—"ready for either or ready for both." I think it is one of the most perfect symbols that I have ever known picturing submission to God's will, and it certainly describes our Lord Jesus Christ.

He was ready first for His labors on earth, the work with the plow; to be followed by the altar of sacrifice. With no side interest, He moved with steady purpose—almost with precision—toward the cross. He would not be distracted nor turned aside. He was completely devoted to the cross, completely devoted to the rescue of mankind, because He was completely devoted to His Father's will!

Even "if we remain not faithful," as the Bible says, that does not change His faithful devotion. He has not changed. He is devoted as He was devoted! He came a devoted One, and the word *devoted* is actually a religious word referring to a sacrifice, usually a lamb that was selected and marked out. It was fed, it was cared for, but everyone considered it already dead on the altar of sacrifice.

It was the lamb that had been selected, and even though it waited in its place a few days, everyone knew of the coming sacrifice. They knew it was devoted. It was an expendable lamb. So, our Lord Jesus Christ was devoted—completely devoted as a lamb to the sacrifice!

Then, the second word is *separation* and the preposition is *from*. Devotion *to* and separation *from*.

There are many ways in which our Lord deliberately separated Himself. He separated Himself *from* men *for* men.

There are those who have separated themselves for other reasons. Timon of Athens, you will remember, turned sour on the human race and went up into the hills, separating himself from mankind because he hated the human race. His separation was the result of hatred. But the separation of Jesus Christ from men was the result of love. He separated Himself from them for them. It was for them He came—and died. It was for them that He arose and ascended and for them appeared at the right hand of God.

This separation from men was not because He was weary of them, nor that He disliked them. Rather, it was because He loved them. It was a separation in order that He might do for them that which they could not do for themselves. He was the only one who could rescue them. So Jesus was a separated man from the affairs of man.

"Separation from" is the phrase that marks Him. He was separated from the net of trivialities. There are so many things that are done in the world by Christians that are not really bad—they are just trivial. They are unworthy, much as if we found Albert Einstein busy cutting out paper dolls. Though deeply disappointed, no one would go to him and say, "Einstein, that's a great sin you are committing." But we would go away shaking our heads and saying, "With a mind like that? One of the six great minds of the ages—cutting paper dolls!"

There are so many trivialities in which great minds seem to engage. Yes, your mind, I mean! Great minds.

You smile and say, "Me?"

Yes, I do mean you!

I mean your mind with its endless capabilities. I mean your spirit with its potential for angelic fellowship and divine communion. Yet we engage in trivialities.

Jesus was never so engaged—He escaped the net of trivialities!

He was separated from sinners, it says in the Bible. He was separated not only from their sins, but separated from their vanities. Vanities. Separated from!

Do I need to remind you in this context that if these words characterized Jesus, they must also characterize each of us who claims to be a follower of Jesus?

Devotion to! Yes, devotion to the Father's will; devotion to the rescue of mankind by the preaching of the gospel; devotion to any necessary sacrifice, having no interests aside, but moving with steady purpose to do the will of God!

Separation from! But not in sourness or contempt, but like the runner, separated from his regular clothing in order that he might strip himself for the race—or like a soldier separated from his civilian garb in order to wear only that which is prescribed to free his arms and legs for combat. It is this separation we must know as His loving disciples.

The third word is *rejection* and this is the phrase of "rejection by."

Plainly, Jesus suffered rejection by mankind because of His holiness. Then He suffered rejection by God because of His sinfulness. But someone will say, "Wait a minute! Would you say our Lord was sinful?"

Yes, vicariously sinful.

He Himself never sinned, but He that knew no sin became sin for us, that we sinners might become the righteousness of God in Him.

In that sense, He suffered a twofold rejection. He was too good to be received by sinful men and in that awful moment of His sacrifice He was too sinful to be received by a holy God. So He hung between heaven and earth rejected by both until He cried, "It is finished. Father, into Thy hand I commend my spirit" (paraphrase of Luke 23:46). Then He was received by the Father.

But while He was bearing my sins and yours, He was rejected by the Father. While He moved among men He was rejected by them because He was so holy that His life was a constant rebuke to them.

Identification with should also be noted. Surely He was identified with us. Everything He did was for us. He acted in our stead. He took our guilt. He gave us His righteousness. In all of these acts on earth, it was for us because by His incarnation, He identified Himself with the human race. In His death and resurrection He was identified with the redeemed human race.

The blessed result is that whatever He is, we are; and where He is, potentially, His people are; and what He is, potentially, His people are—only His deity being excepted!

Finally, consider His *acceptance at.*

Jesus Christ, our Lord, has acceptance at the throne of God. Although once rejected, He is now accepted at—and that bitter rejection is now turning into joyous acceptance. The same is true for His people. Through Him, we died! Identified with Him, we live, and in our identification with Him we are accepted at the right hand of God, the Father.

This is the meaning of our celebration.

REFLECT

1. What are the implications for seeing the church as primarily a communion and not an institution?

2. Tozer claims that we are in "spiritual trouble" if we do not recognize the presence of Christ. What sort of trouble do you think results from not recognizing His nearness?

3. How does Tozer's description of Christ's presence encourage or challenge you?

4. How does knowing that you and all Christians are identified with Christ shape the way you view yourself and other believers?

16

THE SECOND COMING

These have come so that the proven genuineness of your faith—of greater worth than gold, which perishes even though refined by fire—may result in praise, glory and honor when Jesus Christ is revealed.

1 Peter 1:7

Are you ready for the appearing of Jesus Christ or are you among those who are merely curious about His coming?

Let me warn you that many preachers and Bible teachers will answer to God some day for encouraging curious speculations about the return of Christ and failing to stress the necessity for "loving His appearing"!

The Bible does not approve of this modern curiosity that plays with the Scriptures and that seeks only to impress credulous and gullible audiences with the "amazing" prophetic knowledge possessed by the brother who is preaching or teaching!

I cannot think of even one lonely passage in the New Testament which speaks of Christ's revelation, manifestation, appearing, or coming that is not directly linked with moral conduct, faith, and spiritual holiness.

The appearing of the Lord Jesus on this earth once more is not an event upon which we may curiously speculate—and when we do only that we sin. The prophetic teacher who engages in speculation to excite the curiosity of his hearers without providing them with a moral application is sinning even as he preaches.

There have been enough foolish formulas advanced about the return of Christ by those who were simply curious to cause many believers to give the matter no further thought or concern. But Peter said to expect "the appearing of Jesus Christ." Paul said there is a crown of righteousness laid up in glory for all those who love His appearing. John spoke of his hope of seeing Jesus and bluntly wrote: "Every man that hath this hope in him purifieth himself, even as he is pure" (1 John 3:3).

Peter linked the testing of our faith with the coming of the Lord when he wrote of "the trial of your faith, being much more precious than of gold that perisheth, though it be tried with fire, might be found unto praise and honour and glory at the appearing of Jesus Christ" (1 Peter 1:7).

UNDERSTANDING SCRIPTURE

Think of the appearing of Christ; for here is a word that embodies an idea—an idea of such importance to Christian theology and Christian living that we dare not allow it to pass unregarded.

This word occurs frequently in the King James Version of

the Bible in reference to Jesus, and has various forms—such as *appear, appeared, appearing*. The original word from which our English was translated has about seven different forms in the Greek.

But in this usage, we are concerned only with the word *appearing* in its prophetic use. Unquestionably, that is how Peter used it in this passage. Among those seven forms in the Greek there are three particular words that all told may have these meanings: "manifest; shine upon; show; become visible; a disclosure; a coming; a manifestation; a revelation."

I point this out because Peter also wrote that the Christians should "gird up the loins of [their] mind, be sober, and hope to the end for the grace that is to be brought unto you at the revelation of Jesus Christ" (1 Peter 1:13).

Some of you might like to ask the translators a question, but they are all dead! The question might well be, "Why was the similar form of the original word translated in one case as the appearing and in the other as the revelation of Jesus Christ?"

There may have been some very fine shade of meaning that they felt must be expressed by one word and not the other, but we may take it as truth that the words are used interchangeably in the Bible.

We do not have to belabor this point, and actually some people are in trouble in the Scriptures because they try too hard! The Lord never expected us to have to try so hard and to push on to the end of setting up a formula or a doctrinal exposition on the shades of meanings and forms of a single word.

Some of the cults do this. There are prophetic cults whose entire prophetic idea and scheme rest upon the words *appearing* or *revelation* or *manifestation* or *disclosure.* Their leaders write page after page and book after book upon the difference between one shade of meaning and another.

I can only say that I have learned this, having been around for a while—if that cult is forced to belabor a word in order to make a point, check it off and give it no more thought!

If that cult that is obviously a cult with no standing in the historic stream of Christianity and no standing in the long corridor of approved Christian truth tries to build on one word's shade of meanings, you can just shrug it off.

Why do I say that?

Because the Bible is the easiest book in the world to understand—one of the easiest for the spiritual mind but one of the hardest for the carnal mind! I will pay no mind to those who find it necessary to strain at a shade of meaning in order to prove they are right, particularly when that position can be shown to be contrary to all the belief of Christians back to the days of the apostles.

So that is why I say it is very easy to try too hard when we come to the reading and explanation of the Scriptures. You can actually try too hard at almost anything, including baseball.

A certain baseball team, for instance, at the opening of the season tries so hard to win that the players get up-tight, become jittery and jumpy, and they make many errors.

After they find out that they do not really have a chance at the championship, they become relaxed and suddenly they are playing very good baseball. They didn't change any of the men around; they just relaxed and quit pressing so hard!

I think this matter of pushing and trying too hard may also

be of concern to the young preacher getting up before his first audience. His muscles tighten, his throat gets dry, he may not remember his main points—and I have been there myself—pushing; like everything, trying too hard!

But we will never mature in the kingdom of God by pushing and pressing because the kingdom of God is not taken that way. Rather, you trust the Lord and watch Him do it!

The same thing is true concerning interpretation of the Bible. If we insist upon those fine shades of definitions, we may just be trying too hard and we may end up with the wrong point of view!

Perhaps we can illustrate it. Suppose a Chicago man visits his family in Des Moines and after getting back home, writes a number of letters in which he mentions the trip to Iowa.

In one letter he writes, "I visited Des Moines last week."

In a second, he says, "I went to Des Moines last week," and in a third, "I motored to Des Moines last week." In still another, he mentions, "I saw my brother in Des Moines last week."

He seals all of the letters, mails them, and thinks no more of it.

But what would happen if a group of interpreters were turned loose on those five letters after a thousand years, particularly if they were interpreters pushing too hard, insisting that there are no synonyms in the Bible and that the kingdom of God and kingdom of heaven are never used synonymously?

They would make their notes and insist that the writer must have had something special in his mind when he wrote, "I went to Des Moines," and "I motored to Des Moines." Therefore, he must have made at least two trips or he would have said the same thing each time! And then, he must have had some reason for saying in one letter that he visited in Des Moines, which must mean that he stayed longer that time than when he merely saw his brother!

Actually, he was only there once, but in writing, he knew the English language well enough to be able to say it in four different ways.

So, when we come to Peter's use of this word *appearing*—just relax, for that is what it means! If a different form or word is used in another place and the same thing is being stated in a different way, it simply shows that the Holy Ghost has never been in a rut—even if interpreters are! The Spirit of God never has had to resort to clichés even though preachers often seem to specialize in them!

The appearing of Jesus Christ may mean His manifestation. It may mean a shining forth, a showing, a disclosure. Yes, it may mean His coming, the revelation of Jesus Christ!

RETURNING TO EARTH

The question that must actually be answered for most people is: "Where will this appearing or coming or disclosure or revelation take place?"

Those to whom Peter wrote concerning the appearing of Christ were Christian men and women on this earth. There is no way that this can possibly be spiritualized—the scene cannot be transferred to heaven.

Peter was writing to Christians on this earth, to the saints scattered abroad by trial and persecution. He was encouraging them to endure affliction and to trust God in their sufferings, so their faith may be found of more worth than gold at the appearing of Jesus Christ!

Common sense will tell us that this appearing could only be on the earth because he was writing to people on this earth. He was not writing to angels in any heavenly sphere. He was not saying it to Gabriel but to people living on this earth.

Now, Peter also spoke of this as an event to happen in the future, that is, the future from the time in which Peter wrote nineteen centuries ago. Writing in the year AD 65, Peter placed the appearing of Christ sometime in the future after AD 65.

We are sure, then, that Peter was not referring to the appearance of Jesus at the Jordan River when John baptized Him, for that had already taken place thirty years before.

Jesus had also appeared in Jerusalem, walking among the people, talking to the Pharisees and elders, the rabbis and the common people, but that had also taken place thirty years before. He had suddenly appeared in the temple, just when times were good and people were coming from everywhere with money to have it exchanged in order to buy cattle or doves for sacrifice. Using only a rope, He drove the cattle and the money changers from the temple. He appeared on the Mount of Transfiguration and after His resurrection appeared to the disciples. He had made many appearances. He was there in bodily manifestation, and He did things that could be identified. He was there as a man among men. But Peter said, "He is yet to appear" for the other appearances were all thirty years in the past.

Peter was saying: "I want you to get ready in order that the trial of your faith, your afflictions, your obedience, your cross-bearing may mean honor and glory at the appearing of Jesus Christ"—the appearing in the future!

LIKE BEFORE

There is no reputable testimony anywhere that Jesus Christ has appeared since the events when He appeared to put away sin through the sacrifice of Himself.

Actually we haven't found anyone that says Christ appeared to him in person, except some poor fanatic who usually dies later in the mental institution.

Many new cults have arisen; men have walked through the streets saying, "I am Christ." The psychiatrists have written reams and reams of case histories of men who insisted that they were Jesus Christ.

But our Lord Jesus Christ has not yet appeared the second time, for if He had, it would have been consistent with the meaning of the word as it was commonly used in the New Testament. He would have to appear as He appeared in the temple, as He appeared by the Jordan or on the Mount of Transfiguration. It would have to be as He once appeared to His disciples after the resurrection—in visible, human manifestation, having dimension so He could be identified by the human eye and ear and touch.

If the word *appearing* is going to mean what it universally means, the appearing of Jesus Christ has to be very much the same as His appearing on the earth the first time, nearly two thousand years ago.

When He came the first time, He walked among men. He

took babies in His arms. He healed the sick and the afflicted and the lame. He blessed people, ate with them, and walked among them, and the Scriptures tell us that when He appears again He will appear in the same manner. He will be a man again, though a glorified man! He will be a man who can be identified, the same Jesus as He went away.

We must also speak here of the testimonies of Christian saints through the years—if Christ being known to us in spiritual life and understanding and experience.

There is a certain sense in which everyone who has a pure heart "looks upon" God.

There are bound to be those who will say, "Jesus is so real to me that I have seen Him!"

I know what you mean and I thank God for it—that God has illuminated the eyes of your spiritual understanding—and you have seen Him in that sense. "Blessed are the pure in heart: for they shall see God" (Matt. 5:8).

I believe that it is entirely possible for eyes of our faith, the understanding of our spirit, to be so illuminated that we can gaze upon our Lord—perhaps veiled, perhaps not as clearly as in that day to come, but the eyes of our heart see Him!

So, Christ does appear to people in that context. He appears when we pray and we can sense His presence. But that is not what Peter meant in respect to His second appearing upon the earth. Peter's language of that event calls for a shining forth, a revelation, a sudden coming, a visible appearance!

Peter meant the same kind of appearance that the newspapers noted in the appearance of the president of the United States in Chicago. He meant the same kind of appearance that the newspapers noted when the young sergeant appeared suddenly to the delight of his family after having been away for more than two years. There has not been any appearance of Jesus like that since He appeared to put away sins by the sacrifice of Himself!

We can sum this up and say that there is to be an appearance—in person, on earth, according to Peter—to believing persons later than Peter's time. That appearing has not yet occurred and Peter's words are still valid.

We may, therefore, expect Jesus Christ again to appear on earth to living persons as He first appeared.

STRENGTHEN BY THE WORD

The Word of God was never given just to make us curious about our Lord's return to earth, but to strengthen us in faith and spiritual holiness and moral conduct!

When Paul wrote to Timothy in his second letter, we find some of the dearest and most gracious words of the entire Bible:

I charge thee therefore before God, and the Lord Jesus Christ, who shall judge the quick and the dead at his appearing . . . preach the word; be instant in season, out of season; reprove, rebuke, exhort with all long suffering and doctrine. For the time will come when they will not endure sound doctrine. (4:1–3)

Here the apostle cautions that our Lord Jesus Christ will judge the quick and the dead at His appearing, and then he links that appearing and judgment with the earnest exhortation that

Timothy must preach the Word, being instant in season and out of season.

A bit later, Paul writes more about events to happen when Jesus Christ appears.

He wrote: "I have fought a good fight, I have finished my course, I have kept the faith: henceforth there is laid up for me a crown of righteousness, which the Lord, the righteous judge, shall give me at that day: and not to me only, but unto all them also that love his appearing."

It is plainly stated, brethren: those who love the appearing of Jesus Christ are those who shall also receive a crown.

There are some who would like to open this up: "Doesn't it really mean anyone who believes in the premillennial position will receive the crown of righteousness?"

I say no! It means that those who are found loving the appearing of Jesus will receive the crown of righteousness! It is questionable to my mind whether some who hold a premillennial position and can argue for it can be included with those whose spirit of humility and consecration and hunger for God is quietly discernible in their love and expectation of the soon coming of their Savior!

I fear that we have gone to seed on this whole matter of His return. Why is it that such a small proportion of Christian ministers ever feel the necessity to preach a sermon on the truth of His second coming? Why should pastors depend in this matter upon those who travel around the country with their colored charts and their object lessons and their curious interpretations of Bible prophecy?

Should we not dare to believe what the apostle John wrote,

that "we shall be like him; for we shall see him as he is"?

Beloved, we are the sons of God now, for our faith is in the Son of God, Jesus Christ! We believe in Him and we rest upon Him, and yet it doth not yet appear what we shall be; but we know that when He shall appear, when He shall be disclosed, we shall be like Him, for we shall see Him as He is!

Then, John says bluntly and clearly: "Every man that hath this hope in him purifieth himself, even as he is pure." Everybody! Everyone, he says! He singularizes it. Everyone that hath this hope in Him purifies himself as He is pure!

Those who are expecting the Lord Jesus Christ to come and who look for that coming moment by moment and who long for that coming will be busy purifying themselves. They will not be indulging in curious speculations—they will be in preparation, purifying themselves!

It may be helpful to use an illustration here.

A wedding is about to take place and the bride is getting dressed. Her mother is nervous and there are other relatives and helpers who are trying to make sure that the bride is dressed just right!

Why all this helpful interest and concern?

Well, the bride and those around her know that she is about to go out to meet the groom, and everything must be perfectly in order. She even walks cautiously so that nothing gets out of place in dress and veil. She is preparing, for she awaits in loving anticipation and expectation the meeting with this man at the altar.

Now John says, through the Holy Ghost, that he that hath this hope in him purifies and prepares himself. How? Even as He is pure!

The bride wants to be dressed worthy of the bridegroom, and so it is with the groom, as well!

Should not the church of Jesus Christ be dressed worthy of her Bridegroom, even as He is dressed? Pure—even as He is pure?

We are assured that the appearing of Jesus Christ will take place. It will take place in His time. There are many who believe that it can take place soon—that there is not anything that must yet be done in this earth to make possible His coming.

It will be the greatest event in the history of the world, barring His first coming and the events of His death and resurrection.

We may well say that the next greatest event in the history of the world will be "the appearing of Jesus Christ: whom having not seen, ye love; in whom, though now ye see him not, yet believing, ye rejoice with joy unspeakable and full of glory!"

The world will not know it, but he that hath this hope in Him will know it for he has purified himself even as Christ is pure!

REFLECT

1. Do Tozer's words on Christ's second coming line up with what you have thought about it?

2. Are you joyfully anticipating the coming of Christ, or do you find yourself conflicted at times due to earthly desires?

3. Are you preparing for Christ's return? What would it look like for you to prepare?

17

THE HEAD OF NEW CREATION

I am making everything new!

REVELATION 21:5

Only the Christian church in the midst of all the world religions is able to proclaim the Bible's good news that God, the Creator and Redeemer, will bring a new order into being!

Indeed, it is the only good news available to a fallen race today—the news that God has promised a new order that is to be of eternal duration and infused with eternal life.

How amazing!

It is a promise from God of a new order to be based upon the qualities that are the exact opposite of man's universal blight—temporality and mortality!

God promises the qualities of perfection and eternity, which cannot now be found in mankind anywhere on this earth.

What a prospect!

We are instructed that this new order, at God's bidding, will finally show itself in the new heaven and the new earth. It will show itself in the city that is to come down as a bride adorned for her husband.

The Word of God tells us that all of this provision for the redeemed has the quality of eternal duration.

It is not going to come just to go again. It is not to be temporal. It is a new order that will come to stay.

It is not going to come subject to death. It is not to be mortal. It is a new order that will come to live and remain forever!

A NEW MAN, A NEW CREATION

God in His revelation to man makes it very plain that the risen Christ Jesus is the Head of this new creation and that His church is the body. It is a simple picture, instructing us that individual believers in the risen Christ are the body's members.

It seems to me that this is revealed so clearly in the Bible that anyone can see it and comprehend it.

The whole picture is there for us to consider.

The first Adam—the old Adam—was the head of everything in that old order, so when he fell, he pulled everything down with him.

I know that there are some bright human beings who argue against the historicity of the fall of humankind in Adam and Eve. But no man, however brilliant, wise, and well-schooled, has been able to escape two brief sentences written across all of his prospects by the great God Almighty.

Those sentences are: "Man, you cannot stay—you must go!" and "Man, you cannot live—you must die!"

No human being, regardless of talents and possessions and status, has yet won a final victory over his sentence of temporality and mortality.

Temporality says, "You must go!"

Mortality says, "You must die!"

Because this is true, then all of the works that men do actually partake of what man is. The same blight that rests upon sinful, fallen man—namely, temporality and mortality—rests upon every work that man does.

Mankind has many areas of life and culture of which he is proud. Man has long used such words as *beauty*, *nobility*, *creativity*, and *genius*. But all the work of a man's hand, however noble it may be, however inspired by genius, however beautiful and useful—still has these two sentences written across it: "You cannot stay!" and "You cannot live!"

It is still only the work and hope and dream of fallen man and God continually reminds him, "You came only to go and you came surely to die!"

Everything and anything, whether a sonnet or an oratorio, a modern bridge or a great canal, a famous painting or the world's greatest novel—every one has God's mark of judgment upon it. Temporality and mortality!

Not one can remain—it is in the process of going.

Not one is eternal—it is only the work of fallen man who must die. And all of the work that man does cannot escape the sentence of partaking of what man is.

But a second man, the new and last Adam, came into this world to bring the promise of a new and eternal order for God's creation. The Son of Man, Christ Jesus the Lord, came and died, but rising from the grave, lives forever that He might be the Head of the new creation.

God's revelation says that Jesus Christ is the eternal Victor, triumphant over sin and death! That is why He is the Head of the new creation, which has upon it the banner of perfectivity rather than temporality and the mark of life forevermore rather than the mark of death.

WAITING FOR GOD'S PROMISE

When we think of the ebb and flow of man's history and the inability of men to thwart the reality of death and judgment, it seems incredible that proud men and women—both in the church and outside the church—refuse to give heed to the victorious eternal plan and program of Jesus Christ!

Most of the reasons for the neglect of Christ's promises are all too evident among us today.

For one thing, modern man is too impatient to wait for the promises of God. He takes the short-range view of things.

He is surrounded by gadgets that get things done in a hurry. He has been brought up on quick oats; he likes instant coffee, he wears drip-dry shirts, and takes thirty-second Polaroid snapshots of his children.

His wife shops for her spring hat before the leaves fall to the ground in autumn. His new car, if he buys it after July 1, is already an old model when he brings it home.

He is almost always in a hurry and can't bear to wait for anything.

This breathless way of living naturally makes for a mentality impatient of delay, so when this man enters the kingdom of God he brings his short-range psychology with him. He finds prophecy too slow for him. His first radiant expectations soon lose their luster.

He is likely, then, to inquire: "Lord, wilt thou at this time restore again the kingdom to Israel?"

When there is no immediate response, he may conclude, "My Lord delayeth his coming!"

Actually, it has taken some people a long time to discover that the faith of Christ offers no buttons to push for quick service. The new order must wait for the Lord's own time—and that is too much for the man in a hurry.

He just decides to give up and becomes interested in something else.

Also, there is little question that the prevailing affluence of our society has much to do with the general disregard of Christ's promises that He would come to earth again to intervene in human history.

If the rich man enters the kingdom of God with difficulty, then it is logical to conclude that a society having the highest percentage of well-to-do persons in it will have the lowest percentage of Christians, all things else being equal.

If the "deceitfulness of riches" chokes the Word and makes it unfruitful, then this would be the day of near-fruitless preaching, at least in the opulent West.

And if surfeiting and drunkenness and worldly cares tend to unfit the Christian for the coming of Christ, then this generation of Christians should be the least prepared for that event.

On the North American continent, Christianity has become

the religion of the prosperous middle and upper middle classes almost entirely; the very rich or the very poor rarely become practicing Christians.

The touching picture of the poorly dressed, hungry saint, clutching his Bible under his arm and with the light of God shining in his face, hobbling painfully toward the church, is chiefly imaginary.

One of the most irritating problems of even an ardent Christian these days is to find a parking place for the shiny chariot that transports him effortlessly to the house of God where he hopes to prepare his soul for the world to come.

In the United States and Canada, the middle class today possesses more earthly goods and lives in greater luxury than emperors and maharajas did only a century ago.

There surely can be little argument with the assumption that since the bulk of Christians comes from this class, it is not difficult to see why the genuine expectation of Christ's return has all but disappeared from among us.

It is hard indeed to focus attention upon a better world to come when a more comfortable one than this can hardly be imagined. As long as science can make us so cozy in this present world it is admittedly hard to work up much pleasurable anticipation of a new world order even if it is God who has promised it.

BE EXPECTANT

Beyond these conditions in society, however, is the theological problem—too many persons holding an inadequate view of Jesus Christ Himself.

Ours is the age in which Christ has been explained, humanized, demoted. Many professing Christians no longer expect Him to usher in a new order. They are not at all sure that He is able to do so; or if He does, it will be with the help of art, education, science, and technology—that is, with the help of man.

This revised expectation amounts to disillusionment for many. And, of course, no one can become too radiantly happy over a King of kings who has been stripped of His crown or a Lord of lords who has lost His sovereignty.

Another facet of the problem is the continuing confusion among teachers of prophecy, some of whom seem to profess to know more than the prophets they claim to teach.

This may be in the realm of history, but it was only a little more than a short generation ago, around the time of the first World War, that there was a feeling among gospel Christians that the end of the age was near and there was anticipation and hope of a new world order about to emerge.

In the general outline of the scriptural hope, this new order was to be preceded by a silent return of Christ to earth, not to remain, but to raise the righteous dead to immortality and to glorify the living saints in the twinkling of an eye. These He would catch away to the marriage supper of the Lamb, while the earth meanwhile plunged into its baptism of fire and blood in the Great Tribulation. This would be relatively brief, ending dramatically with the battle of Armageddon and the triumphant return of Christ with His Bride to reign a thousand years.

Let me assure you that those expectant Christians had something very wonderful, which is largely lacking today. They had a unifying hope. Their activities were concentrated. They fully expected to win.

Today, our Christian hope has been subjected to so much examination, analysis, and revision that we are embarrassed to admit that we believe there is genuine substance to the hope we espouse.

Today, professing Christians are on the defensive, trying to prove things that a previous generation never doubted. We have allowed unbelievers to get us in a corner and have given them the advantage by permitting them to choose the time and place of encounter.

We smart under the attack of the quasi-Christian unbeliever, and the nervous, self-conscious defense we make is called "the religious dialogue."

Under the scornful attack of the religious critic, real Christians, who ought to know better, are now "rethinking" their faith.

Worst of all, adoration has given way to celebration in the holy place, if indeed any holy place remains to this generation of confused Christians.

In summary, I think that we must note that there is a vast difference between the doctrine of Christ's coming and the hope of His coming.

It surely is possible to hold the doctrine without feeling a trace of the blessed hope. Indeed there are multitudes of Christians today who hold the doctrine—but what I have tried to deal with here is that overwhelming sense of anticipation that lifts the life upward to a new plane and fills the heart with rapturous optimism. It is my opinion that this is largely lacking among us now.

Frankly, I do not know whether or not it is possible to recapture the spirit of anticipation that animated the early Christian church and cheered the hearts of gospel Christians only a few decades ago.

Certainly scolding will not bring it back, nor arguing over minor points of prophecy, nor condemning those who do not agree with us. We may do all or any of these things without arousing the desired spirit of joyous expectation. That unifying, healing, purifying hope is for the childlike, the innocent-hearted, the unsophisticated.

Brethren, let me tell you finally that all those expectant believers in the past have not been wholly wrong. They were only wrong about the time. They saw Christ's triumph as being nearer than it was, and for that reason their timing was off; but their hope itself was valid.

Many of us have had the experience of misjudging the distance of a mountain toward which we were traveling. The huge bulk that loomed against the sky seemed very near, and it was hard to persuade ourselves that it was not receding as we approached.

So the City of God appears so large to the minds of the world-weary pilgrim that he is sometimes the innocent victim of an optical illusion; and he may be more than a little disappointed when the glory seems to move farther away as he approaches.

But the mountain is really there—the traveler need only press on to reach it. And the Christian's hope is substance too; his judgment is not always too sharp, but he is not mistaken in the long view—he will see the glory in God's own time!

REFLECT

1. How would knowing that Christ is the Head of new creation inform the way you live your life now?

2. Have you "demoted" Christ in your mind compared to how Tozer portrays Him in this chapter?

3. Reflecting on the pace of your life, do you find that you are fixed on eternity, or are you concerned primarily with concerns of the now?

4. What do you imagine the church today would look like if it were as expectant as the early church was for Christ's new order?

REFERENCES

Chapter 1: The Self-Existent God
Christ the Eternal Son (Camp Hill, PA: Christian Publications, 1982; repr. Chicago, IL: WingSpread Publishers, 2010), 30–42.

Chapter 2: God's Express Image
Jesus, Our Man in Glory (Camp Hill, PA: Christian Publications, 1987; repr. Chicago, IL: WingSpread Publishers, 2009), 34–44.

Chapter 3: Creator, Sustainer, Benefactor
Christ the Eternal Son, 18–25, 27–29.

Chapter 4: The Revelation of God
Jesus, Our Man in Glory, 17–23.

Chapter 5: The Mystery of the Incarnation
Christ the Eternal Son, 7–16.

Chapter 6: The Center of All
Tozer Speaks, Volume 2 (Camp Hill, PA: Christian Publications, 1994; repr. Camp Hill, PA: WingSpread Publishers, 2010), 389–96.

Chapter 7: Miracle Worker
Jesus, Our Man in Glory, 60–66.

Chapter 8: The People's Savior
Christ the Eternal Son, 101–108.

Chapter 9: The Remedy
Tozer Speaks, Volume 2, 386–89, 395–96.

Chapter 10: The Offering
Attributes of God, Volume 1 (Camp Hill, PA: Christian Publications, 2003; repr. Chicago, IL: WingSpread Publishers, 2007), 67–74.

Chapter 11: Our Mediator
Jesus, Our Man in Glory, 121–26.

Chapter 12: The Resurrection
Tozer Speaks, Volume 2, 411–20.

Chapter 13: The Ascended Lord
Jesus, Our Man in Glory, 78–81; *Warfare of the Spirit* (Camp Hill, PA: Christian Publications, 1193; repr. Chicago, IL: WingSpread Publishers, 2006), 115–19.

The Tozer Essentials

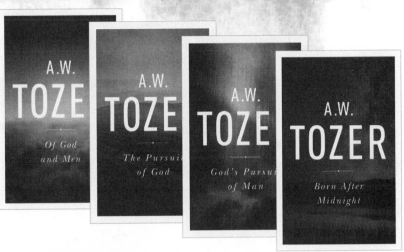

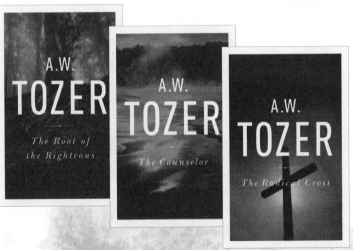

MOODY
Publishers™

From the Word to Life

Two 365-Day Devotionals
by A. W. Tozer

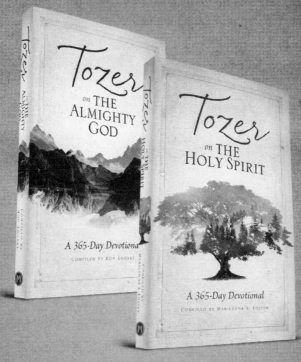

DWELL ON THE AWESOMENESS OF THE ALMIGHTY GOD AND UNEARTH THE WONDER OF THE HOLY SPIRIT WITH THESE TWO DEVOTIONALS.

Tozer was a man who walked closely with God, who prayed often and shunned distraction so he could gaze more purely upon Him. Tozer was also a man who thirsted for the Spirit of God, who prayed often and shunned distraction so that he might drink Him in more steadily. In these daily meditations on Scripture, Tozer will inspire you to do the same.

MOODY
Publishers™

From the Word to Life

TITLES BY A.W. TOZER

The Attributes of God, Volume I

The Attributes of God, Volume II

The Best of A. W. Tozer, Book One

The Best of A. W. Tozer, Book Two

Born After Midnight

The Christian Book of Mystical Verse

Christ the Eternal Son

The Counselor

The Early Tozer: A Word in Season

Echoes from Eden

Evenings with Tozer

Faith Beyond Reason

Gems from Tozer

God Tells the Man Who Cares

God's Pursuit of Man (formerly *Pursuit of Man* and *Divine Conquest*)

How to Be Filled with the Holy Spirit

I Call It Heresy!

I Talk Back to the Devil

Jesus, Author of Our Faith

Jesus Is Victor

Jesus, Our Man in Glory

Let My People Go, A biography of Robert A. Jaffray

Man: The Dwelling Place of God

Men Who Met God

Mornings with Tozer

The Next Chapter After the Last

Of God and Men

Paths to Power

The Price of Neglect

The Pursuit of God

The Pursuit of God: A 31-Day Experience

The Radical Cross

The Root of the Righteous

Rut, Rot or Revival

The Set of the Sail

The Size of the Soul

Success and the Christian

That Incredible Christian

This World: Playground or Battleground?

Tozer on the Almighty God

Tozer for the Christian Leader

Tozer on the Holy Spirit

Tozer on Worship and Entertainment

Tozer Speaks (in two volumes)

Tozer Speaks to Students

Tragedy in the Church: The Missing Gifts

The Warfare of the Spirit

We Travel an Appointed Way

Whatever Happened to Worship?

Who Put Jesus on the Cross?

Wingspread, a biography of A. B. Simpson

From the Word to Life

Moody Radio produces and delivers compelling programs filled with biblical insights and creative expressions of faith that help you take the next step in your relationship with Christ.

You can hear Moody Radio on 36 stations and more than 1,500 radio outlets across the U.S. and Canada. Or listen on your smartphone with the Moody Radio app!

www.moodyradio.org